Really Useful Home Book

Robert Frederick
Publishers

This Edition © Robert Frederick Publishers
©Text and Illustrations
First Edition 2000
4 & 5 North Parade Bath England

INDEX

INDEX

Name ....

Address ....

Tel.: Home ....

     Business ....

     Car ....

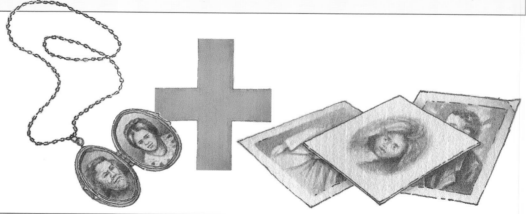

In Case of Emergency

Contact ....

Telephone No. ....

Blood Group ....

Known Allergies ....

Useful Telephone Numbers

Accountant	....	Optician	....
Airport	....	Plumber	....
Bank	....	Railway Station	....
Building Society	....	Solicitor	....
Club	....	Taxi/Car Hire	....
Dentist	....	Travel Agent	....
Doctor	....	Vet	....
Electrician	....	Water	....
Gas	....	Other	....

Useful Information

National Insurance No.	....	Car Key No.	....
Passport No.	....	Car Insurance Policy No.	....
Driving License No.	....	Renewal Date	....
Credit Card No.s	....	AA/RAC Membership No.	....

Notes

....

....

....

PERSONAL TELEPHONE NUMBERS

Name .... ☎ ....

Name .... ☎ ....

Name .... ☎ ....

Name .... ☎ ....

Name .... ☎ ....

Name .... ☎ ....

Name .... ☎ ....

Name .... ☎ ....

Name .... ☎ ....

Name .... ☎ ....

Name .... ☎ ....

Name .... ☎ ....

Name .... ☎ ....

Name .... ☎ ....

Name .... ☎ ....

Name .... ☎ ....

Name .... ☎ ....

Name .... ☎ ....

Name .... ☎ ....

Name .... ☎ ....

Name .... ☎ ....

Name .... ☎ ....

THINGS TO REMEMBER

Use this space to note down renewal dates for Television License,
Road Tax, MOT, Insurance policies etc.

BIRTH SIGNS

ARIES (March 21-April 20)

Fiery First Sign

Symbol: The Ram

Ruling Planet: Mars

Birthstone: Diamond

Flower: Sweet Pea

Colours: Fiery Red, Orange

Numbers: Seven, Six

Day: Tuesday

CANCER (June 22-July 22)

Watery Fourth Sign

Symbol: Crab, Moon

Ruling Planet: The Moon

Birthstone: Moonstone, Pearl

Flower: Larkspur

Colours: Silver, Sea Green

Numbers: Eight, Three

Day: Friday

LIBRA (Sept. 23-Oct. 23)

Airy Sociable Seventh Sign

Symbol: The Scales

Ruling Planet: Venus

Birthstone: Opal

Flower: Calendula

Colour: Peacock Blue

Numbers: Six, Nine

Day: Friday

CAPRICORN (Dec. 24-Jan. 20)

Earthy Tenth Sign

Symbol: The Goat

Ruling Planet: Saturn

Birthstone: Garnet

Flower: Carnation

Colours: Restrained to Dark

Numbers: Seven, Three

Day: Saturday

TAURUS (April 21-May 21)

Earthy Second Sign

Symbol: The Bull

Ruling Planet: Venus

Birthstone: Emerald

Flower: Lily of the Valley

Colours: Natural colours

Numbers: One, Nine

Day: Friday

LEO (July 23-August 23)

Fiery & Fixed Fifth Sign

Symbol: The Sun, The Lion

Ruling Planet: The Sun

Birthstone: Sardonyx

Flower: Gladioli

Colours: Gold, Fiery Shades

Numbers: Five, Nine

Day: Sunday

SCORPIO (Oct. 24-Nov. 22)

Watery Eighth Sign

Symbol: The Scorpion

Ruling Planet: Mars

Birthstone: Topaz

Flower: Chrysanthemum

Colours: Dark Water Shades

Numbers: Three, Five

Day: Tuesday

AQUARIUS (Jan. 21-Feb. 18)

Airy, Stubborn Eleventh Sign

Symbol: Water Carrier

Ruling Planet: Uranus

Birthstone: Amethyst

Flower: Violet

Colours: Wild, Way Out

Numbers: Eight, Four

Day: Wednesday

GEMINI (May 22-June 21)

Airy Third Sign

Symbol: The Twins

Ruling Planet: Mercury

Birthstone: Agate

Flower: Rose

Colours: Sky Blue, Black

Numbers: Three, Four

Day: Wednesday

VIRGO (August 24-Sept. 22)

Earthy & Adaptable Sixth Sign

Symbol: Fertility Goddess

Ruling Planet: Mercury

Birthstone: Sapphire

Flower: Aster

Colours: Natural, Warm

Numbers: Eight, Four

Day: Wednesday

SAGITTARIUS (Nov. 23-Dec. 23)

Fiery, Adaptable Ninth Sign

Symbol: The Archer

Ruling Planet: Jupiter

Birthstone: Turquoise

Flower: Narcissus

Colours: Fiery Reds

Number: Nine

Day: Thursday

PISCES (Feb. 19-March 20)

Watery, Compromising Twelfth Sign

Symbol: Two Fish

Ruling Planet: Neptune

Birthstone: Bloodstone

Flower: Jonquil

Colours: Violet, Oceanic

Numbers: Five, Eight

Day: Friday

BIRTHDAYS

Spouse ....

Children ....

....

....

....

Grandchildren

....

....

....

....

....

....

Mother ....

Father ....

Mother-in-law ....

Father-in-law ....

Brothers & Sisters ....

....

....

....

....

Other Family ....

....

....

....

....

Friends

....

....

....

....

....

....

Miscellaneous

....

....

....

....

....

....

....

ANNIVERSARIES

....

....

....

....

....

....

....

....

....

....

....

"It is not the years in your life but the life in
your years that counts!"

Adlai Stevenson: Coronet

~ WEDDING ANNIVERSARIES ~

First	Paper	Tenth	Tin	Thirtieth	Pearl
Second	Cotton	Eleventh	Steel	Thirty-fifth	Coral
Third	Leather	Twelfth	Silk, Linen	Forty-fifth	Sapphire
Fourth	Fruit, Flowers	Thirteenth	Lace	Fortieth	Ruby
Fifth	Wood	Fourteenth	Ivory	Fiftieth	Gold
Sixth	Sugar, Iron	Fifteenth	Crystal	Fifty-fifth	Emerald
Seventh	Wool, Copper	Twentieth	China	Sixtieth	Diamond
Eighth	Bronze, Pottery	Twenty-fifth	Silver	Seventieth	Platinum
Ninth	Pottery, Willow			Seventy-fifth	Diamond

SPECIAL OCCASIONS

Occasion .... Date ....

Occasion .... Date ....

Occasion .... Date ....

Occasion .... Date ....

Occasion .... Date ....

Occasion .... Date ....

Occasion .... Date ....

Occasion .... Date ....

Occasion .... Date ....

Occasion .... Date ....

Occasion .... Date ....

Occasion .... Date ....

Occasion .... Date ....

"All who joy would win
Must share it, -
Happiness was born a Twin."

Byron: Don Juan

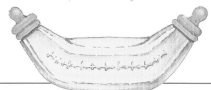

QUOTATIONS FOR SPECIAL OCCASIONS

ABSENCE/PARTING

"Sometimes when one person
is missing, the whole world
seems depopulated."

Lamartine

"To leave is to die a little;
It is to die to what one loves.
One leaves behind a little of oneself
At any hour, any place."

Edmond Haraucourt

"The joys of meeting pay
the pangs of absence;
Else who could bear it?"

Nicholas Rowe

BEREAVEMENT

"Pain lays not its touch
Upon a corpse."

Aeschylus

"He who has gone, so we but
cherish his memory, abides with us,
more potent, nay, more present,
than the living man."

Saint-Exupéry

BIRTHS

"We find delight in the beauty
and happiness of children
that makes the heart too big
for the body."

Ralph Waldo Emerson

"Children are poor men's riches."

English Proverb

"There never was child so lovely
but his mother was glad to
get him asleep."

Ralph Waldo Emerson

"Life's aspirations come in
the guise of children."

Rabindranath Tagore

"Adam and Eve had many
advantages but the principal one
was that they escaped teething."

Mark Twain

"A sweet child is the sweetest
thing in nature."

Charles Lamb

Everyday Thoughts
for everyday living

"They are able because
they think they are able."

Virgil

"Natural ability without education
has oftener raised men to glory
and virtue, than education without natural
ability."

Cicero

"Our hours in love have wings;
in absence crutches."

Colley Cibber

"Absence diminishes moderate passions
and increases great ones,
as the wind extinguishes tapers and adds
fury to fire."

François de la Rochefoucauld

"He knows not his own strength
that hath not met adversity."

Ben Jonson

- Name

Name

Name

Name

Name

Name

QUOTATIONS FOR SPECIAL OCCASIONS

BIRTHDAYS

"First you forget names, then you forget faces, then you forget to pull your zipper up, then you forget to pull your zipper down."

Lee Rosenburg

"Whenever a man's friends begin to compliment him about looking young, he may be sure that they think he is growing old."

Washington Irving

"Unto each man comes a day when his favourite sins all forsake him, And he complacently thinks he has forsaken his sins."

John Hay

"How beautiful is youth! how bright it gleams With its illusions, aspirations, dreams."

Longfellow

"It's not that age brings childhood back again, Age merely shows what children we remain."

Goethe: Faust

BIRTHDAYS

"What [Time] hath scanted men in hair, he hath given them in wit."

Shakespeare: The Comedy of Errors

"It isn't how long you stick around but what you put over while you are here."

George Ade

"Middle age is when your age starts to show around the middle."

Bob Hope

"To me, old age is always fifteen years older than I am."

Bernard Baruch

"Old men like to give good advice in order to console themselves for not being any longer able to set bad examples."

François de la Rochefoucauld

"Growing old is no more than a bad habit which a busy man has no time to form."

André Maurois

"There is nothing which we receive with so much reluctance as advice."

Joseph Addison

"Age only matters when one is aging. Now that I have arrived at a great age. I might just as well be twenty."

Picasso

"Aim at the sun, and you may not reach it; but your arrow will fly far higher than if aimed at an object on a level with yourself."

J Hawes

"He that is slow to anger is better than the mighty; and he that ruleth his spirit than he that taketh a city."

Proverbs 16:32

"The only way to get the best of an argument is to avoid it."

Dale Carnegie

Addresses · Addresses · Addresses · Addresses · Addresses · Addresses

A

Name
✉

☎
Name
✉

☎
Name
✉

☎
Name
✉

☎
Name
✉

☎
Name
✉

☎
Name
✉

☎

QUOTATIONS FOR SPECIAL OCCASIONS

CONSOLATION

"Let us remember, when we are inclined to be disheartened, that the private soldier is a poor judge of the fortunes of a great battle."

W R Inge

"It's not how far you fall, but how high you bounce."

Author Unidentified

"When the One Great Scorer comes to write against your name, He marks, not that you won or lost, but how you played the game."

Grantland Rice

COURAGE

"Don't be afraid to take big steps. You can't cross a chasm in two small jumps."

David Lloyd George

"What matters is not the size of the dog in the fight, but the size of the fight in the dog."

Coach Bear Bryant

DIFFICULT TIMES

"Human misery must somewhere have a stop: there is no wind that always blows a storm."

Euripides

"God will not look you over for medals, degrees or diplomas, but for scars."

Elbert Hubbard

"The worse the passage the more welcome the port."

Thomas Fuller

EDUCATION

"An investment in knowledge always pays the best interest."

Benjamin Franklin

"Education is an ornament in prosperity and a refuge in adversity."

Aristotle

"Learning without thought is labour lost; thought without learning is perilous."

Confucius

Everyday Thoughts
for everyday living

"Every baby born into the world
is a finer one than the last."

Charles Dickens: Nicholas Nickleby

"A baby is an angel whose wings decrease
as his legs increase."

French Proverb

" A beautiful face is of all spectacles the
most beautiful."

Jean de la Bruyère

"Achieving starts with believing."

Author Unidentified

"A man lives by believing something: not
by debating and arguing
about many things."

Thomas Carlyle

B

Name
✉

☎ Name
✉

☎ Name
✉

☎ Name
✉

☎ Name
✉

☎ Name
✉

☎

QUOTATIONS FOR SPECIAL OCCASIONS

FAMILY

"To forget one's ancestors is to be
a brook without a source,
a tree without a root."

Chinese Proverb

"When brothers agree, no fortress
is so strong as their common life."

Antisthenes

"God could not be everywhere,
so He made mothers."

Jewish Proverb

"Mother is the name for God in the
lips and hearts of little children."

W M Thackeray: Vanity Fair

"When I was a boy of fourteen, my
father was so ignorant I could hardly
stand to have the old man around.
But when I got to be twenty one,
I was astonished at how much
he had learned in seven years."

Mark Twain

"A father is a banker by nature."

French Proverb

FRIENDSHIP

"There's nothing worth
the wear of winning,
But laughter and the
love of friends."

Hilaire Belloc

"A friend may well be reckoned
the masterpiece of nature."

Ralph Waldo Emerson

"We do not mind our not arriving
anywhere nearly so much as our not
having any company on the way."

Frank Moore Colby

HAPPINESS

"Silence is the perfectest herald
of joy. I were but little happy if
I could say how much."

Shakespeare: Much Ado About Nothing

"Grief can take care of itself,
but to get the full value of joy
you must have somebody to
divide it with."

Mark Twain

Everyday Thoughts
for everyday living

"Burdens become light when
cheerfully borne."

Author Unidentified

"Whenever you see a successful
business, someone once made
a courageous decision."

Peter Drucker

"To business that we love
we rise betime,
And go to't with delight."

Shakespeare: Anthony and Cleopatra

"Few people do business well
who do nothing else."

Lord Chesterfield

"The busier we are, the more acutely we
feel that we live, the more conscious we
are of life."

Immanuel Kant

B

Name

✉

☎

Name

✉

☎

Name

✉

☎

Name

✉

☎

Name

✉

☎

Name

✉

☎

QUOTATIONS FOR SPECIAL OCCASIONS

HOUSE-WARMING

"You are a king by your own fire-side, as much as any monarch in his throne."

Cervantes

"A man's home is his wife's castle."

Alexander Chase

LOVE

"Love, all alike, no season knows, nor clime,
Nor hours, age, months, which are the rags of time."

John Donne

"One word
Frees us of all the weight and pain of life:
That word is love."

Sophocles

"All love is sweet,
Given or returned.
Common as light is love,
And its familiar voice wearies not ever."

Shelley

RETIREMENT

"Cessation of work is not accompanied by cessation of expenses."

Cato the Elder

"Dismiss the old horse in good time, lest he fail in the lists and the spectators laugh."

Horace

"To the art of working well a civilised race would add the art of playing well."

George Santayana

REUNIONS

"A man's real possession is his memory. In nothing else is he rich, in nothing else is he poor."

Alexander Smith

"To be able to enjoy one's past life is to live twice."

Martial

"Bliss in possession will not last;
Remembered joys are never past."

James Montgomery

Everyday Thoughts
for everyday living

"Challenges can be stepping stones or stumbling blocks. It's just a matter of how you view them."

Author Unidentified

"Wondrous is the strength of cheerfulness, and its power of endurance - the cheerful man will do more in the same time, will do it better, will persevere in it longer than the sad or sullen."

Thomas Carlyle

"Of cheerfulness, or a good temper - the more it is spent, the more of it remains."

Ralph Waldo Emerson

"Children are the true connoisseurs. What's precious to them has no price, only value."

Bel Kaufman

Name

✉

☎

Name

✉

☎

Name

✉

☎

Name

✉

☎

Name

✉

☎

Name

✉

☎

QUOTATIONS FOR SPECIAL OCCASIONS

SUFFERING

"A Wounded Deer – leaps highest."

Emily Dickinson

"We are healed of a suffering only by experiencing it to the full."

Marcel Proust

"Sadness flies on the wings of the morning and out of the heart of darkness comes the light."

Jean Giraudoux

TRAVEL

"The less a tourist knows, the fewer mistakes he need make, for he will not expect himself to explain ignorance."

Henry Adams

"He who would travel happily must travel light."

Saint-Exupéry

"He that travels much knows much."

Thomas Fuller

WEDDINGS

"An ideal wife is any woman who has an ideal husband."

Booth Tarkington

"A man's wife has more power over him than the state has."

Ralph Waldo Emerson

"Any married man should forget his mistakes – no use two people remembering the same thing."

Duane Dewel

"Only two things are necessary to keep one's wife happy. One is to let her think she is having her own way, and the other, to let her have it."

Lyndon B Johnson

"Marriage is popular because it combines the maximum of temptation with the maximum of opportunity."

Shelley

"One of the best hearing aids a man can have is an attentive wife."

Groucho Marx

Everyday Thoughts
for everyday living

"Blessed be childhood, which brings down something of heaven into the midst of our rough earthliness."

Henri Frédéric Amiel

"An agreeable companion on a journey is as good as a carriage."

Publilius Syrus

"What value has compassion that does not take its object in its arms?"

Saint-Exupéry

"Worse than idle is compassion
If it ends in tears and sighs."

William Wordsworth

"Content makes poor men rich;
discontent makes rich men poor."

Benjamin Franklin

Addresses • Addresses • Addresses • Addresses • Addresses • Addresses • Addresses

Name

Name

Name

Name

Name

Name

IN THE KITCHEN ~ WEIGHTS, MEASURES & TEMPERATURES

COOKING (DIAL MARKINGS)

Gasmark	¼	1	2	3	4
Fahrenheit	250	275	300	325	350
Celsius	120	140	150	160	180

Gasmark	5	6	7	8	9
Fahrenheit	375	400	425	450	475
Celsius	190	200	220	230	240

OVEN TEMPERATURES

Gasmark	Description
¼	Very Slow
½	Very Slow
1	Slow
2	Slow
3	Moderate
4	Moderate
5	Moderately Hot
6	Moderately Hot
7	Hot
8	Hot
9	Very Hot

Conversions given are approximate.
Never mix metric and imperial measures in one recipe - stick to one system or the other.

TEMPERATURE CONVERSION CHART

°F	°C
212B	100B
122	50
113	45
104	40
95	35
86	30
77	25
68	20
59	15
50	10
41	5
32	0
23	-5
14	-10
5	-15
-4	-20

DRY WEIGHT

Approximate gram conversion to nearest round figure	Recommended gram conversion to nearest 25g	Imperial ounce (oz)	
28	25	1	
57	50	2	
85	75	3	
113	100-125	4	(¼lb)
142	150	5	
170	175	6	
198	200	7	
227	225	8	(½lb)
255	250	9	
284	275	10	
311	300	11	
340	350	12	(¾lb)
368	375	13	
396	400	14	
425	425	15	
453	450	16	(1lb)

LIQUID MEASURES

Approx. mililitre conversion to nearest round figure	Recommended mililitre equivalent	Imperial pint	Imperial fluid ounce (oz)
568	575-600	1	20
284	300	½	10
142	150	¼	5

Everyday Thoughts
for everyday living

"It is always darkest just before
the day dawneth."

Thomas Fuller

"To die completely, a person must not only
forget but be forgotten, and he who is not
forgotten is not dead."

Samuel Butler

"Oh, what a tangled web we weave
When first we practice to deceive."

Walter Scott: Marmion

"Despair exaggerates not only
our misery but also our weakness."

Luc de Vauvenargues

"Despair of nothing.
[Nil desperandum]."

Latin Proverb

D

Name
✉

☎
Name
✉

☎
Name
✉

☎
Name
✉

☎
Name
✉

☎
Name
✉

☎

FOOD & HEALTH ~ Calorie Expenditure

Below are given the approximate energy costs of some activities for a 70 kg adult:

Activity	Calories used per 15 min	Activity	Calories used per 15 min
Sitting	20	Energetic dancing	85
Sweeping	30	Judo, karate, tai'chi	90
Sitting, writing	35	Skating, roller skating	90
Sailing	40	Playing cricket - batting	100
Driving a car	48	Playing tennis	120
Table tennis	50	Jogging	120
Yoga	50	Digging	130
Walking slowly	55		
Ironing	60		
Cycling slowly	65		
Surfing/wind surfing	65		
Polishing the floor	68		
Water skiing	70		
Badminton	70	Playing football	140
		Shovelling earth	160
		Cycling fast	168
		Skiing downhill	175
		Climbing with a pack	200
		Running	200
		Squash	230
Golf	75	Swimming fast	255
Walking fast	80	Skiing cross-country	280
Ballet	80		

Everyday Thoughts
for everyday living

"Difficulties strengthen the mind,
as labour does the body."
Seneca

"The best way out of a difficulty
is through it."
Author Unidentified

"What we hope to do with ease, we must
first learn to do with diligence."
Samuel Johnson

"Our duty is to be useful,
not according to our desires,
but according to our powers."
Henri Frédérick Amiel

"The path of duty lies in the thing that
is nearby, but men seek it
in things far off."
Chinese Proverb

Name
✉

☎
Name
✉

☎
Name
✉

☎
Name
✉

☎
Name
✉

☎
Name
✉

☎

FOOD & HEALTH ~ Calorie Counting

Calories per ounce (25g) unless otherwise stated:		
Anchovies	40	
Apples	10	
Apricots		
Canned in syrup	30	
Dried	50	
Fresh, with stone	5	
Artichokes (boiled)	5	
Asparagus	5	
Aubergines	5	
Sliced & fried (1oz raw)	60	
Avocado Pears (flesh only)	65	
Bacon		
Back raw	120	
Streaky raw	115	
Bananas (flesh only)	20	
Bass (steamed fillet)	35	
Bean Sprouts (raw)	10	
Beans		
Baked beans	20	
Broad (boiled)	15	
Butter (boiled)	25	
French (boiled)	neg	
Haricot (boiled)	30	
Kidney (canned)	25	
Runner (boiled)	5	
Soya (raw, dried)	115	
Beef		
Brisket (boiled)	90	
Minced beef (raw)	75	
Minced beef (1oz raw, well fried & drained of fat)	45	
Rump steak (fried, lean)	55	
Rump steak (grilled, lean)	50	
Sirloin (roast, lean & fat)	50	
Stewing steak (raw)	50	
Topside (roast, lean & fat)	60	
Beetroot (boiled)	15	
Blackberries (fresh)	10	
Blackcurrants (fresh)	10	
Black Pudding (raw)	105	
Bran	60	
Bread		
Brown/Wheatmeal/Hovis/White	65	

Malt	70	
Wholemeal	60	
Bap (50g)	120	
Croissant (50g)	270	
Crusty roll	145	
French Bread (50g)	130	
Granary	70	
Hot cross bun (50g)	180	
Pitta bread (45g)	125	
Rye bread	70	
Tea cake (50g)	155	
Broccoli (boiled)	5	
Brussels Sprouts (boiled)	5	
Butter	210	
Cabbage (boiled)	5	
Carrots (boiled)	5	
Cauliflower (boiled)	5	
Caviar	75	
Celery	neg	
Cheese		
Austrian Smoked	80	
Babybel	95	
Blue Stilton	130	
Boursin	115	
Brie	90	
Cairphilly	120	
Camembert	90	
Cheddar	120	
Cheshire	110	
Cottage Cheese	25	
Cream Cheese	125	
Curd Cheese	40	
Danish Blue	105	
Danish Mozzarella	100	
Double Gloucester	105	
Edam	90	
Emmenthal	115	
Gorgonzola	110	
Gouda (not matured)	95	
Gruyere	130	
Lancashire	110	
Leicester	105	
Norwegian Blue	100	
Parmesan	115	
Processed	90	
Rambol (with walnuts)	115	

Roquefort	90
Sage Derby	110
Wensleydale	115
White Stilton	95
Cherries	
Fresh with stones	10
Glace	60
Chicken	
On bone, raw	25
Meat only, raw	40
Meat & skin, roast	60
Chinese Leaves	neg
Chives	10
Chocolate	
Milk/Plain	150
Cooking	155
Cod	
On bone, raw	15
Fillet, raw	20
Fried in batter	55
Steamed fillet	25
Coffee (instant)	30
Corned Beef	60
Corn o/t Cob (boiled, kernels only)	35
Courgettes	5
Cream	
Clotted	165
Double	125
Single	60
Soured	55
Whipping	95
Cucumber	5
Currants	70
Dates (per date)	15
Duck	
Roast, meat only	55
Roast, meat, fat & skin	95

28

Everyday Thoughts
for everyday living

"Early rising not only gives us more life in the same number of years, but adds, likewise, to their number."

Charles Cotton

"Education is what survives when what has been learnt has been forgotten."

B F Skinner

"Education is an ornament in prosperity and a refuge in adversity."

Aristotle

"Correction does much, but encouragement does more."

Johann Wolfgang von Goethe

"Love your enemies, bless them that curse you, do good to them that hate you, and pray for them which despitefully use you, and persecute you."

Matthew 5:44

Name
✉

☎
Name
✉

☎
Name
✉

☎
Name
✉

☎
Name
✉

☎
Name
✉

☎

Eggs		
Graded Eggs	Raw	Fried
1	95	145
2	90	140
3	80	130
4	75	120
5	70	110
6	60	100
Yolk of size 3 egg		60
White of size 3 egg		15
Gherkins		5
Gooseberries (fresh, dessert)		10
Grapefruit		
Canned in syrup		15
Flesh only/With skin		5
Juice		10
Grapes		15
Haddock		
On bone, raw		15
Fillet, raw		20
On bone, smoked		20
Smoked fillet		30
Fried fillet in breadcrumbs		50
Hake		
On bone, raw		10
Fillet, raw		20
Fillet, steamed		30
Fillet, fried		60
Halibut		
On bone, steamed		30
Fillet, steamed		35
Ham		
Lean, boiled		60
Fatty, boiled		120
Herring		
On bone, grilled		40
Fillet, grilled		55
Honey		80
Ice-cream		45
Jam		75
Kidney (raw)		25
Kippers (baked or grilled fillet)		60
Lamb		
Roast breast, boned,		115
Roast breast, boned, lean only		75
Roast leg, boned,		75

Roast leg, boned, lean only	55
Roast shoulder, lean & fat	90
Roast shoulder, lean only	55
Leeks (raw)	10
Lemon Sole	
On bone (grilled or steamed)	20
Fillet (grilled or steamed)	25
Lentils (boiled)	30
Lettuce (raw)	5
Liver	
Chicken's, fried	55
Lamb's, fried	65
Ox, stewed	55
Pig's, stewed	55
Liver sausage	90
Lobster	
With shell, boiled	10
Meat only, boiled	35
Macaroni (boiled)	35
Mackerel	
On bone, fried	40
Fillet, fried	55
Smoked	70
Mandarins	
Canned	15
Fresh, with skin	5
Margarine	205
Marmalade	75
Marzipan	125
Mayonnaise	205
Melon (with skin)	5
Milk	
Gold Top	430
Red Top	370
Longlife/UHT	370
Low-fat powdered	200
Pasteurised/SIlver Top	370
Skimmed	200
Sterilized	370
Evaporated	45
Condensed (sweetened)	90
Muesli	105
Mushrooms (raw)	5
Mussels	
Boiled, with shells	5
Boiled, without shells	25

Nectarines	15
Noodles (cooked) 35Nuts (mixed, roasted, salted)	175
Olive Oil	255
Olives (with stones, in brine)	25
Onions	
Raw	5
Fried	100
Rings fried in batter	145
Oranges	
Flesh only	10
With skin	5
Juice	10
Parsnips (raw or boiled)	15
Peaches	
Fresh, with stones	10
Canned in syrup	25
Peanuts	
Shelled or roasted, salted	160
Peanut butter	175
Pears	
Fresh	10
Canned in syrup	20
Peas	
Fresh, raw	20
Fresh, boiled	15
Canned, garden	15

Canned, processed	25
Chick, raw	90
Perch	
White	35
Yellow	25
Pheasant	
Roast, on bone	40
Roast, meat only	60

Everyday Thoughts
for everyday living

"Let age, not envy, draw wrinkles
on thy cheeks."

Sir Thomas Browne

"The quality of a person's life is in direct
proportion to their commitment to
excellence, regardless of their chosen field
of endeavour."

Vince Lombardi

"He that is good for making excuses
is seldom good for anything else."

Benjamin Franklin

"Experience is not what happens
to you; it is what you do with
what happens to you."

Aldous Huxley

"To most men, experience is like the stern
lights of a ship, which illumine only the
track it has passed."

S T Coleridge

Addresses • Addresses • Addresses • Addresses • Addresses

Name
✉

☎
Name
✉

☎
Name
✉

☎
Name
✉

☎
Name
✉

☎
Name
✉

☎

Pilchards (canned in tomato sauce)	35
Pineapples	
Fresh	15
Canned in syrup	20
Plaice (fillet)	
Raw or steamed	25
Fried in batter	80
Fried in crumbs	65
Plums	
Fresh dessert, with stones	10
Cooking, with stones	5
Pork	
Roast, lean & fat	80
Roast, lean meat only	50
Cracking	190
Scratchings	185
Prawns	
With shells	10
Without shells	30
Prunes	
Dried	45
Stewed (no sugar)	25
Rabbit	
On bone, stewed	25
Meat only, stewed	50
Radishes	5
Raspberries	
Fresh	5
Tinned, drained	25
Redcurrants (fresh)	5
Rhubarb	neg
Rice	
Raw	100
Boiled	35
Salmon	
Raw, on bone	50
Steamed, on bone	45

Steamed, fillet	55
Canned	45
Smoked	40
Sardines	
Canned in oil, drained	60
Canned in tomato sauce	50
Sausages	
Pork, lightly fried or grilled	165
Pork, well fried or grilled	115
Pork, chipolata:	
lightly fried or grilled	165
well fried or grilled	115
Beef, fried or grilled	120
Beef, chipolata fried or grilled	120
Scampi (fried in breadcrumbs)	90
Semolina (raw)	100
Shrimps	
With shells	10
Without shells	35
Canned	25
Skate (fillet fried in batter)	55
Sole	
Fillet, raw	25
Fillet, fried	60
Fillet, steamed	25
On bone, steamed	20
Spaghetti	
Raw	105
Boiled	35
Canned in tomato sauce	15
Spinach (boiled)	10
Spring Onions	10
Strawberries	
Fresh	5
Tinned, drained	25
Sturgeon (on bone, raw)	25
Sugar	110
Sultanas (dried)	70
Sunflower Seed Oil	255
Swedes	5
Sweetcorn	
Canned	20
Fresh boiled, kernels	35
Frozen	25
Sweets	
Boiled sweets	95

Filled chocolates	130
Fudge	110
Peppermints	110
Toffee	120
Syrup	
Golden	85
Maple	70
Tangerines	
Flesh only	10
With skin	5
Tapioca (dry)	100
Tea	neg
Tomatoes	
Canned	5
Fried, halved	20
Fried, sliced	30
Ketchup	30
Puree	20
Raw	5
Tongue (Ox, boiled)	85
Treacle (Black)	85
Tripe (Stewed)	30
Trout	
Fillet, smoked	35
On bone, steamed	25
Tuna	
Canned in oil	80
Drained of oil	60
Turkey	
Meat only, roast	40
Meat & skin, roast	50
Turnips (raw)	5
Veal	
Escalope, fried (egg/b'crumbs)	60
Fillet, raw	30
Fillet, roast	65
Venison (roast, meat)	55
Watermelon	5
Whitebait (fried)	150
Whiting	
On bone, fried	50
Fillet, fried	55
On bone, steamed	20
Fillet, steamed	25
Yorkshire Pudding (cooked)	60

'neg' signifies negligible calorie content

Everyday Thoughts
for everyday living

"If your life is free of failures,
you're not taking enough risks."
Author Unidentified

"There is no failure except in
no longer trying."
Elbert Hubbard

"Only the person who has faith in himself
is able to be faithful to others."
Erich Fromm

"The greatest of faults is to be
conscious of none."
Thomas Carlyle

"Present fears are less than
horrible imaginings."
Shakespeare: Macbeth

F

Name
✉

☎
Name
✉

☎
Name
✉

☎
Name
✉

☎
Name
✉

☎
Name
✉

☎

IN THE KITCHEN ~ Vegetables

Cooking Times & Methods of Some Vegetables

Vegetable	Steam	Boil	Bake (Whole)	Braise	Stir Fry
Asparagus		10-15 mins			
Beetroot		40-60 mins			
Broad Beans		10-15 mins			
Broccoli	4-8 mins				yes
Brussels Sprouts	6-10 mins		25-30 mins		yes
Cabbage	4-6 mins				yes
Carrots	20 mins	10-15 mins	45-60 mins	15-20 mins	yes
Cauliflower	4-8 mins				
Celery	12-15 mins	8-10 mins		10-12 mins	yes
Chicory					yes
Chinese Leaves	4 mins				yes
Courgettes	4-8 mins				yes
Cucumbers	5-10 mins				
Endive				10-12 mins	
Fennel	12-15 mins	10-12 mins		15-20 mins	yes
French Beans	4-8 mins				yes
Globe Artichokes		30-40 mins			
Jerusalem Artichokes		15-20 mins			
Leeks	15-20 mins	10-15 mins		8-10 mins	
Mangetout Peas	6-8 mins				yes
Marrow	10-12 mins		45-60 mins		yes
Mushrooms					yes
Okra		15-20 mins			
Onions			45-60 mins		
Parsnips		15-20 mins	45-60 mins	15-20 mins	
Peas		8-12 mins			yes
Peppers					yes
Potatoes	25-30 mins	20 mins	1-1½ hours	15-20 mins	
Radish/Daikon					yes
Red Cabbage				45-60 mins	
Swedes	25-30 mins	20 mins		15-20 mins	yes
Sweet Potato	25-30 mins	20 mins	1-1½ hours		
Sweetcorn		8-15 mins			yes
Turnips	25-30 mins	10-15 mins		15-20 mins	yes

These are suggestions only and will give very lightly cooked vegetables. Increase the cooking time for softer vegetables. The freshness of the vegetables may also affect the cooking time.

Everyday Thoughts
for everyday living

"The only thing we have to fear
is fear itself."

F D Roosevelt

"Forgiveness is the answer to the child's
dream of a miracle by which what is
broken is made whole again, what is soiled
is again made clean."

Dag Hammarskjold

"I keep my friends as misers do their
treasure, because, of all the things granted
us by wisdom, none is greater or better
than friendship."

Pietro Aretino

"A true friend is the greatest
of all blessings."

François de la Rochefoucauld

"Generosity gives assitance
rather than advice."

Luc de Vauvenargues

F

Name

✉

☎

Name

✉

☎

Name

✉

☎

Name

✉

☎

Name

✉

☎

Name

✉

☎

IN THE KITCHEN ~ Herbs & Spices

HERBS

Herbs play an essential role in any kitchen, adding flavour and distinction to many dishes. All are available fresh or dried but remember that fresh herbs have a milder flavour and use roughly 15ml (1 tablespoon) of fresh herbs to 5ml (1 teaspoon) of dried.

Basil (Ocimum basilicum)

Two types of basil are grown; sweet and bush. The one most commonly found is sweet basil, which has largish, shiny, green leaves and a strong but sweet flavour. It is one of the best herbs to add to tomatoes, eggs, mushrooms and pasta dishes, forms part of a classic bouquet garni, and is an essential part of pesto sauce. Basil does not dry very successfully.

Bay Leaves (Laurus nobilis)

Sweet bay or bay laurel is a Mediterranean tree. The leaves are shiny, smooth and dark with a strong aromatic scent. It is often added to stocks when poaching fish, or to marinades, casseroles, soups and stews. It can also be used to flavour milk puddings.

Chervil (Anthriscus cerefolium)

Chervil is a member of the parsley family and is very popular with French chefs. It has a delicate fern-like leaf, offering a delicate taste with a hint of anise. It is especially good in soups, egg and cheese dishes, or added for flavour to green salad. It can also be used as a garnishing leaf.

Chives (Allium schoenoprasum)

A member of the onion family, chives have a mild onion flavour and long, spiky, green leaves. Raw chives are frequently used in salads, but can be added to omelettes, cheese dishes, and, mixed with soured cream, used as a topping for baked potatoes.

Coriander (Coriandrum sativum)

Coriander has flat feathery leaves and is often confused with flat parsley. It has a distinctive spicy flavour and is popular in Southern European, Indian and South East Asian cooking. The leaves are chopped and added to curries, stews, soups and marinades. It is also known as Chinese or Japanese parsley, and is used in the same way as parsley.

Dill (Anethum graveolens)

A delicate, feathery herb with an aromatic, sharp but sweet flavour. One of the most popular herbs in Scandinavia, it is especially good with fish if added to the marinade, cooking liquid or accompanying sauces. It can also be added to vegetables, cream or cottage cheese.

Lemon Balm (Melissa officinalis)

The crushed leaves of this plant, as the name would suggest, give off a wonderful lemony scent, making them ideal for use in salads.

Marjoram (Origanum majorana)

Sweet marjoram, a plant native to the Mediterranean, has small, furry leaves and a flavour similar to oregano but sweeter and milder. It can be added to most savoury dishes and is good with marrow, potatoes and rice. It is very fragrant and can be dried successfully.

Everyday Thoughts
for everyday living

"Genius is 1 per cent inspiration
and 99 per cent perspiration."

Thomas A Edison

"Nothing is so strong as gentleness, and
nothing is so gentle as real strength."

Ralph W Sockman

"The great mind knows the
power of gentleness,
Only tries force because persuasion fails."

Robert Browning

"Grace is the absence of everything that
indicates pain or difficulty, hesitation or
incongruity."

William Hazlitt

Name

✉

☎

Name

✉

☎

Name

✉

☎

Name

✉

☎

Name

✉

☎

Name

✉

☎

Mint (Menta spp.)

There are many species of this popular herb, from spearmint to the fresh-tasting peppermint used for tisanes. It is probably the best known herb in Britain and most commonly used with lamb and new potatoes. It can also be added to other young vegetables or chopped with minced beef, or mixed with yogurt for a dip. It also combines well with fruit.

Oregano (Origanum vulgare)

Oregano is wild marjoram, and, as it has the best flavour when grown in strong sun, is popular in Mediterranean cuisines - especially those of Italy and Greece. The flavour is similar to marjoram but stronger and the leaves are larger and darker. It enhances many meat dishes and it is often added to salads, pizza and tomato based dishes. Oregano can be dried successfully, keeping all its aroma.

Parsley (Petroselinum crispum)

There are two types of parsley: curled and flat. Flat (or French) parsley is generally grown in Europe and is considered to have a finer taste than curled parsley, but both are strong in Vitamin C and iron. Parsley is an essential part of a bouquet garni. It enlivens most savoury dishes and is often simply used as a garnish, either chopped or as sprigs. The chopped leaves can be added to salads, soups, sauces and cooked vegetables. It is said that if chewed after eating garlic it will remove the smell.

Rosemary (Rosmarinus officinalis)

A pungent, fragrant shrub with small, narrow leaves, set densely on the branches. It is often used with lamb but can be used with other meats and in vegetable dishes such as ratatouille or added to marinades.

Sage (Salvia officinalis)

Sage comes in many varieties and is a strongly flavoured herb with narrow, pale grey-green leaves with a rough texture. It has traditionally been used with pork, liver, and in stuffing, but can be used with any richly flavoured meat, and in cheese and tomato dishes. It dries well but can become musty if kept too long.

Savory (Satureja)

There are two varieties of savory: Winter savory (Satureja montana), and Summer savory (Satureja hortensis). The German name for winter savory means "bean-herb", indicating its traditional use, while summer savory is similar and even more aromatic.

Tarragon (Artemisia dracunculus)

There are two varieties of this herb: French and Russian. The French variety is harder to grow but is far more aromatic than the Russian. It has a distinctive flavour and shiny narrow leaves. It is widely used in vinegars, soups, stuffings, sauces, and salad dressings, and is also good with roast meat, poultry dishes and fish.

Thyme (Thymus vulgaris)

This popular herb contains an essential oil, thymol, which helps to digest fatty foods. Its small, dark-green bushy leaves have a very strong flavour. It is another herb which should be used in a bouquet garni, and it can be used to flavour meat, fish, soups, stews and vegetables.

Everyday Thoughts
for everyday living

"Gratitude is the heart's memory."

French Proverb

"No metaphysician ever felt the deficiency of language so much as the grateful."

C C Colton

"A grateful mind, by owing owes not, but still pays, at once Indebted and discharged."

Milton: Paradise Lost

"Gratefulness is the poor man's payment."

English Proverb

"The only cure for grief is action."

G H Lewes

"Nothing speaks our grief so well As to speak nothing."

Richard Crashaw

39

Addresses · Addresses · Addresses · Addresses

Name

✉

☎

Name

✉

☎

Name

✉

☎

Name

✉

☎

Name

✉

☎

Name

✉

☎

SPICES

Spices are the dried parts of aromatic plants and may be the fruit, root, flower, bud, bark or seed. For the best flavour, grind your own spices just before use.

Aniseed (Pimpinella asinum)

Aniseed has a strong liquorice flavour and is popular in Mexico and all over the Mediterranean.

Capers (Capparis spinosa)

The buds of a small Mediterranean bush, these are usually sold pickled in vinegar and should not be allowed to dry out. While they are used mostly in sauces and salads, they are also popular as a pizza topping, adding an authentic Mediterranean flavour.

Caraway (Carum carvi)

Caraway is in appearance similar to cumin seed and because of this is often confused with it. The taste, however, is very different.

Cardamom (Elettaria cardamomum)

Cardamom is a relative of the ginger family, available both whole green, black or white or ground. The most common is the grey-green pod which contains minute, dark brown seeds with an unmistakable bitter-sweet flavour with a hint of lemon and eucalyptus. It is used extensively in sweet and savoury Indian cookery as well as in Europe and the Middle East for cakes, biscuits and pickles and to flavour drinks.

Chili (Capsicum frutescens)

Ripe chili peppers dry and keep well and are most commonly used in chili powder, a very hot spice, whose blend may vary due to the numerous varieties of chilies to be found. Cayenne is a very hot, pungent red chili sold ready ground. Milder chili powders can be found or you can use chili seasoning which is a blend of ground dried chilis with other spices. It is used (sparingly) in meat, fish, poultry and egg dishes as well as soups, sauces and pickles.

Cinnamon (Cinnamomum zeylanicum)

The distinctive sticks of dried bark are harvested from the young shoots of a large, tropical evergreen. While it is best purchased as sticks and used whole or ground, is also available as a powder and has a sweet pungent flavour. Cinnamon is usually added to savoury dishes in the East and to sweet dishes in the West, and is used in apple desserts, cakes and mulled drinks.

Cloves (Eugenia caryophyllata)

Cloves are the unopened flower buds of the tropical evergreen clove tree. They become rich brown in colour when dried and resemble small nails in shape. Cloves have a penetrating taste and are available whole or ground: if used whole then they are best removed before a dish is eaten. They are used mainly to flavour fruit dishes, mulled wine, mincemeat, bread sauce and curries.

Coriander (Coriandrum sativum)

Coriander is a member of the parsley family. The aromatic brown seeds have a sweet orangey flavour. Sold whole or ground, they are quite mild so can be used more freely than most spices and are used widely in Arab and Eastern cookery; in curries, casseroles, soups, dishes such as couscous and hummus and with vegetables and chutneys.

Everyday Thoughts
for everyday living

"We first make our habits,
and then our habits make us."

Author Unidentified

"Success is getting what you want.
Happiness is liking what you get."

Author Unidentified

"Happiness makes up in height for
what it lacks in length."

Robert Frost

"We have no more right to consume
happiness without producing it than to
consume wealth without producing it."

George Bernard Shaw

"When I was at home, I was in
a better place."

Shakespeare: As You Like It

41

Name
✉

☎
Name
✉

☎
Name
✉

☎
Name
✉

☎
Name
✉

☎
Name
✉

☎

Addresses • Addresses • Addresses • Addresses • Addresses

Cumin (Cuminum cyminum)

Cumin is a member of the parsley family and is available both as seeds or in powdered form. It has a sharp, spicy, slightly bitter taste and should be used in moderation. It is often combined with coriander as a basic curry mixture, but is also used for flavouring Middle Eastern fish recipes, casseroles and couscous. It can be added to pickles, chutneys, soups and rice dishes.

Ginger (Zingiber officinale)

Ginger is a distinctive knobbly root with a hot sweetish taste sold in several forms. Fresh root ginger, essential for many Eastern recipes, releases its true flavour on cooking. It is peeled and then sliced or grated for use in curries, Chinese cooking or marinades for meat, fish and poultry. Dried ginger is the dried ground root and is best used in preserves, cakes, biscuits and puddings. Stem ginger is available preserved in syrup or crystallized and is a sweetmeat either eaten whole, with carel, or used in breads, cakes, confectionery and desserts.

Juniper (Juniperus communis)

Juniper berries have a pungent, slightly resinous flavour. They go well with cabbage and add a light touch to oily or heavy dishes.

Mace (Myristica fragrans)

Mace is the dried outer membrane of nutmeg. It is sold both as blades or ground, although ground mace quickly loses its flavour. It is used in mulled wines and punches, meat pies, loaves, stews, savoury white sauces and in milk puddings.

Nutmeg (Myristica fragrans)

Nutmeg has a brown uneven outer surface with a pale interior, is milder than mace although slightly nuttier and is available whole or ground, but as it loses its flavour quickly, is best grated as required. It can be sprinkled on vegetables and is used in soups, sauces, meat terrines, pates, and puddings.

Paprika (Capsicum annum)

A finely ground red powder made from the fruits of several chili plants, popular in Hungary and Spain. The flesh only is used for mild sweet paprikas whilst the seeds are included in more pungent paprikas. Use to add colour to egg and cheese dishes, in salads, with fish and shellfish, chicken and classically in Hungarian Goulash.

Saffron (Crocus sativus)

Saffron is the dried stigmas of the saffron crocus flower. It is very expensive, as it is individually handpicked and imparts a slightly bitter honey-like flavour and a yellow colour. It is safer to buy the threads as the powder is easy to adulterate. It is added to rice dishes, Spanish Paella, Bouillabaisse and to Cornish Saffron cake.

Turmeric (Circuma longa)

Turmeric is the dried root of a plant from the ginger family, usually sold ground, although sometimes sold fresh. It has a strong woody aroma and a slightly bitter flavour and is used to colour rice, pickles, cakes and in curries and dhals. It is sometimes used as a cheap substitute for saffron to colour dishes, but the flavour is not the same.

Vanilla (Vanilla planifolia)

Vanilla is the fruit of an orchid plant found in Mexico. It has traditionally been used to flavour chocolate, and is good in many sweet dishes, though it is expensive to buy.

Everyday Thoughts
for everyday living

"We should not let our fears hold us back from pursuing our hopes."

John F Kennedy

"The hope set before us . . . is like an anchor for our lives, an anchor safe and sure."

Hebrews 6.19

"When there is room in the heart there is room in the house."

Danish Proverb

"Hospitality is to be shown even towards an enemy. The tree doth not withdraw its shade, even from the woodcutter."

The Hitopadesa

"Better is it to be of a humble spirit with the lowly than to divide the spoil with the proud."

Proverbs 16:19

H

Name
✉

☎
Name
✉

☎
Name
✉

☎
Name
✉

☎
Name
✉

☎
Name
✉

☎

FROM TURKEY

CACIK

Ingredients

1 cucumber	2-3 cloves garlic
$^3/_4$ pint yogurt	3 tbsp chopped mint
salt, white pepper	

Method

Peel & dice cucumber, then sprinkle with salt and leave in colander for half an hour. Crush garlic with a little salt, add to yogurt and mix well. Add salt, pepper and mint, drain cucumber and stir in. Garnish with mint.

IMAM BAYILDI

Ingredients

3 large onions	3 large aubergines (with leaf bases cut off)
olive oil	1 clove garlic
12 oz tomatoes	1 tbsp chopped parsley
$^1/_2$ tsp cinnamon	1 heaped tbsp finely chopped pine kernels (optional)
1 tsp castor sugar	salt, black pepper

Method

Wipe the aubergines and put in large saucepan. Add boiling water and cover. Cook for 10 mins, drain, then plunge into cold water. Leave for 5 mins, cut in half lengthways, scoop out most of flesh, leaving half-inch thick shells. Arrange shells in buttered overproof dish and sprinkle with salt and pepper. Pour 4 tbsp olive oil into each shell and cook, uncovered, in pre-heated oven (350°F or equivalent) for 30 mins. While aubergines are cooking, peel and finely chop onions, skin and chop tomatoes and crush garlic. Heat 2 tbsp of oil in a frying pan, add onions and garlic and fry gently for 5 mins, then add tomatoes, cinnamon, sugar and parsley; season to taste. Simmer until liquid has reduced by half (about 20 mins). Chop aubergine flesh and add to frying pan with pine kernels and cook for 10 mins. Remove aubergine shells from oven, stuff with tomato mixture and serve hot or cold.

TURKISH YOGURT

Ingredients

2 cartons natural yogurt	1 tbsp lemon juice
1 tsp castor sugar	1 tsp lemon rind
2 oz seedless raisins	1 tbsp desiccated coconut

Method

Mix all ingredients together, put in covered dish and chill. Leave to stand for at least one hour before serving to allow flavour to develop.

Everyday Thoughts
for everyday living

"Man's mind once stretched by a new idea, never regains its original dimension."

Oliver Wendell Holmes

"Idleness, like kisses, to be sweet must be stolen."

Jerome K Jerome

"There is always hope in a man who actually and earnestly works. In idleness alone is there perpetual despair."

Thomas Carlyle

"The man with imagination is never alone."

Author Unidentified

"By asking for the impossible we obtain the best possible."

Italian Proverb

Name

Name

Name

Name

Name

Name

FROM GREECE

TARAMASALATA

Ingredients

8 oz smoked cod roe (fresh or tinned)
6-8 tbsp olive oil

juice of 1 large lemon
black pepper

Method

Place roe in a mixing bowl. Add oil and lemon juice alternately, a little at a time, and beat vigorously after each addition until the mixture is a creamy paté. Season to taste with freshly ground black pepper and pack into a dish. Cover and chill lightly. Serve with hot crisp toast, unsalted butter, black olives and lemon wedges.

DOLMADES

Ingredients

12 fresh vine/cabbage leaves or a 7 oz tin of vine leaves
1 lb lean lamb, minced
1 onion
4 oz long grain rice
3 oz butter
1 ½ pints of white stock

1 dsp chopped fresh mint or parsley
1 tsp powdered rosemary
salt, black pepper
juice of half a lemon
5 fl oz yogurt

Method

Peel onion and chop finely. Melt 1 oz butter and fry onion and rice until lightly coloured. Add enough stock to cover rice and cook over low heat until tender, stirring frequently. Leave to cool. Stir in minced lamb, herbs and salt and pepper. Blanch the fresh vine or cabbage leaves for a few minutes in boiling water, spread out and put a spoonful of lamb and rice filling on each; fold the leaves over to make small, neat parcels. Pack carefully in layers in casserole pan. Put a plate on top to keep the parcels under the liquid. Cover and simmer for one hour. Serve yogurt separately.

HISTORIAN'S PUDDING

Ingredients

2 oz self-raising flour
4 oz fresh breadcrumbs
4 oz suet
8 oz raisins
1 tbsp allspice
1 tbsp milk

1 oz sugar
2 chopped dried figs
grated rind of ½ lemon
2 eggs, beaten
2 tbsp sherry

Method

Mix all dry ingredients together. Stir in eggs and sherry, then add milk to make a soft dough. Put in buttered pudding basin and cover with foil. Steam for 3-4 hours and serve hot with sherry sauce.

Everyday Thoughts
for everyday living

"Nature knows no pause in her progress and development, and attaches her curse on all inaction."

Johann Wolfgang von Goethe

"He's armed without that's innocent within."

Alexander Pope

"A man is not to aim at innocence any more than he is to aim at hair, but he is to keep it."

Ralph Waldo Emerson

"A moment's insight is sometimes worth a life's experience."

Oliver Wendell Holmes

"Instinct is intelligence incapable of selfconciousness."

John Sterling

I

Name
✉

☎
Name
✉

☎
Name
✉

☎
Name
✉

☎
Name
✉

☎
Name
✉

☎

IN THE KITCHEN ~ International Recipes

FROM AMERICA

TUNA WALDORF SALAD

Ingredients

2 7-oz tins of tuna	$1/4$ cup walnuts
1 cup diced apples	$1/2$ cup mayonnaise
$1/2$ cup chopped celery	lettuce
crumbled blue cheese	

Method

Drain and flake the tuna. In a bowl combine all ingredients except lettuce and blue cheese. Mix well. Serve on lettuce leaves. Garnish with crumbled blue cheese.

SLOPPY JOES

Ingredients

1 lb minced beef	2 tsp cloves
1 large onion	2 tsp white sugar
1 green pepper	2 tsp vinegar
2 tbsp American mustard	tomato ketchup
1 tsp brown sugar	10 bread rolls

Method

Chop the onion and the green pepper and fry the meat until it is brown. Then add the rest of the ingredients. Mix together and fry for about 10 minutes. 'Slop' onto hamburger style buns.

PUMPKIN PIE

Ingredients

For the Pastry:

6 oz plain flour	4 oz soft brown sugar
3 oz butter	1 tsp cinnamon
milk or water	1 tsp mace
pinch of salt	$1/4$ tsp ground nutmeg

For the Filling:

1 14-oz tin pumpkin (or fresh pumpkin)	$1 1/2$ tsp salt
$1/4$ pint milk	$1/4$ pint single cream
2 eggs, lightly beaten	

Method

Preheat oven to 450°F. Prepare blind pastry shell but do not bake it. Combine all the filling ingredients, mixing well. Pour into the pie crust. Bake in oven for 15 mins, then lower temperature to 350°F and bake till firm - about another 50 mins. Serve warm or cold with grated cheese on top or with cream.

Everyday Thoughts
for everyday living

"Though jealousy be produced
by love, as ashes are by fire,
yet jealousy extinguishes love
as ashes smother the flame."

Margaret of Navarre

"It is not love that is blind, but jealousy."

Lawrence Durrell

"Jealousy: that dragon which slays love
under the pretense of keeping it alive."

Havelock Ellis

"A wise man sings his joy
in the closet of his heart."

Tibullus

"All who joy would win
Must share it, -
Happiness was born a Twin."

Byron: Don Juan

Addresses • Addresses • Addresses • Addresses • Addresses

Name
✉

☎
Name
✉

☎
Name
✉

☎
Name
✉

☎
Name
✉

☎
Name
✉

☎

FROM FRANCE

FRENCH ONION SOUP

Ingredients

2 oz butter or margarine

2 large onions

2 pints of stock

sliced French bread

grated Gruyère cheese

seasoning

Method

Slice onion thinly and fry in butter, add the stock and simmer for about 30 minutes. Season with salt and pepper. Meanwhile, sprinkle cheese on bread slices and brown under a hot grill. Put bread in bottom of soup bowls and pour soup on top.

QUICHE LORRAINE

Ingredients

8 oz shortcrust pastry

1 onion

4 rashers bacon

1 small leek, chopped

$^1/_4$ pint milk

3 eggs

2 oz grated cheese

seasoning

Method

Make pastry and with it line a deep 7-inch sandwich tin, or a flan ring or a 1 pint deep ovenproof plate. Chop the onion and bacon into small pieces and then fry in margarine until tender. Turn them into the pastry case. Beat eggs, stir in the milk, seasoning and most of the cheese, and add the chopped leek. Pour this mixture into the case, sprinkle rest of cheese on top. Bake the flan until it is just set and golden brown on top, 350°F or Gas Mark 5 for 35-40 minutes.

FRENCH CUSTARD ICE CREAM

Ingredients

2 large eggs

$^1/_2$ pint single cream

3 tbsp granulated sugar

2 tsp vanilla essence

Method

Set fridge to its coldest setting one hour before making ice cream. Place cream, eggs and sugar into a double saucepan with water simmering. Sitr continuously until the custard is thick enough to coat thinly the back of a spoon. Do not let it boil. Pour into a bowl, stir in the vanilla essence and cool. Pour when cold into ice cube tray and place in the freezer section of your fridge. Freeze until ice cream has frozen about $^1/_2$ inch round sides of tray (about 1 hour). Turn into chilled bowl and whisk until smooth. Return to washed and dried tray and freeze until firm (a further $1^1/_2$ to 2 hours).

Everyday Thoughts
for everyday living

"He who binds to himself a joy
Does the winged life destroy;
But he who kisses the joy as it flies
Lives in eternity's sunrise."

William Blake

"Joy is for all men. It does not depend on
circumstance or condition: if it did, it
could only be for the few."

Horace Bushnell

"If you judge, investigate."
[Si judicas, cognosce.]

Seneca

"He hath a good judgement that relieth
not wholly on his own."

Thomas Fuller

"Extreme justice is often unjust."

Racine

51

Addresses · Addresses · Addresses · Addresses · Addresses · Addresses

Name
✉

☎
Name
✉

☎
Name
✉

☎
Name
✉

☎
Name
✉

☎
Name
✉

☎

IN THE KITCHEN ~ International Recipes

FROM JAPAN

NABEMONO (COD SOUP)

Ingredients

2 fillets cod	12 mushrooms
3 leeks	2 packets bean cake (available from health food shops)
Chinese leaves or spinach	soy sauce

Method

Cut cod into small pieces and cut bean cake into cubes. Wash vegetables and put water in large saucepan. When hot but not boiling, add fish and bean cake. Bring to boil and skim off froth. Add all the vegetables. Simmer for 10 minutes.

TAKIKOMI GOHAN (CHICKEN RICE)

Ingredients

4 cups pudding rice	1 carrot
3 tbsp saki or white wine	3 mushrooms
soy sauce	$1/4$ chicken
1 pinch salt	$1/2$ lb french beans

Method

Wash rice until the water is clear and leave to drain for 30 minutes. Slice carrot and mushrooms and cut chicken into very small pieces. Put about $4 1/2$ cups of water in saucepan, add rice and all ingredients except the beans. Bring to boil on high heat then remove lid. Leave boiling hard for 2 minutes. When water is almost gone and air holes appear in rice, turn heat down very low. Meanwhile boil french beans very lightly in salted water. Chop up with butter and mix with rice before serving.

YAKITOR (CHICKEN)

Ingredients

4 chicken pieces	ground ginger
soy sauce	1 red chili
saki or white wine	1 garlic clove

Method

Chop chili and garlic and wash chicken. Put all ingredients in dish and leave overnight, turning occasionally. Before the meal, grill the chicken.

This can be served with raw vegetables or salad, cucumber, tomatoes, chopped cabbage, grated carrots, lettuce etc.

Everyday Thoughts
for everyday living

"You can accomplish by kindness what you cannot do by force."

Publilius Syrus

"One who knows how to show and to accept kindness will be a friend better than any possession."

Sophocles

"I expect to pass through life but once. If, therefore, there be any kindness I can show, or any good thing I can do for any fellow being, let me do it now, for I shall not pass this way again."

William Penn

"The smallest act of kindness is worth more than the grandest intention."

Author Unidentified

Name

✉

☎

Name

✉

☎

Name

✉

☎

Name

✉

☎

Name

✉

☎

Name

✉

☎

Addresses • Addresses • Addresses • Addresses • Addresses

IN THE KITCHEN ~ International Recipes

FROM ITALY

SPAGHETTI BOLOGNESE

Ingredients

1 onion	$^1/_4$ lb mushrooms
1 $^1/_2$ oz butter	5oz tin tomato purée
1 dsp olive oil	2 tsp sugar
$^1/_2$ lb minced beef	$^1/_2$ tsp mixed herbs
$^1/_2$ pint water	$^3/_4$ lb spaghetti
4 oz cheddar cheese	seasoning
1 garlic clove	Bay leaf

Method

Chop onion and fry gently, add meat and fry for 4 minutes, stirring. Add chopped garlic and sliced mushrooms together with water, sugar, bay leaf, tomato purée, herbs and seasoning. Bring to boil and simmer for 30 minutes, stirring often. Boil spaghetti for 20 minutes in salted water. Drain and serve with sauce and finely grated cheese.

RISOTTO MILANESE

Ingredients

1 small onion	$^3/_4$ lb long grain rice
3 oz butter	3 oz cheese
1 $^1/_2$ pints chicken stock	seasoning

Method

Fry chopped onion gently in 2 oz butter. Add rice and fry for 1 minute, stirring Gradually add hot stock. Simmer in covered pan for 25 minutes, stirring often. Add 1 oz butter and 1 oz cheese. Serve with grated cheese.

MILANESE SOUFFLE

Ingredients

2 lemons	$^1/_2$ oz gelatine
3 eggs, separated	5 tbsp water
4 oz sugar	chopped nuts, whipped cream, glacé cherries & angelica
$^1/_2$ pint double cream	(for decoration)

Method

Dissolve gelatine in water, using bowl in saucepan of warm water. To another bowl in warm water add egg yolks, sugar, juice and grated rinds from lemons, whisking until thick and creamy. Remove from heat and whisk until the outside of the bowl is cold. Fold in lightly whipped cream, then add whisked egg whites and finally the gelatine. Pour mixture into souffle case and chill. Stand on large plate and decorate with chopped nuts, whipped cream, glacé cherries and angelica.

Everyday Thoughts
for everyday living

"A kiss can be a comma, a question mark
or an exclamation point.
That's basic spelling that every woman
ought to know."

Mistinguett

"We owe almost all our knowledge,
not to those who have agreed,
but to those who have differed."

C C Colton

"To know that we know what
we know, and that we do not know what
we do not know,
that is true knowledge."

Henry David Thoreau

"As we acquire more knowledge,
things do not become more
comprehensible, but more mysterious."

Albert Schweitzer

K

Name

✉

☎

Name

✉

☎

Name

✉

☎

Name

✉

☎

Name

✉

☎

Name

✉

☎

FROM HUNGARY

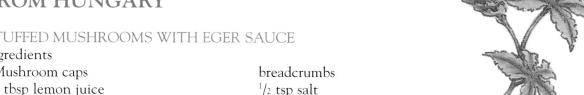

STUFFED MUSHROOMS WITH EGER SAUCE

Ingredients

Mushroom caps

1 tbsp lemon juice

goose liver paté (or similar)

beaten egg

breadcrumbs

$^1/_2$ tsp salt

deep fat or oil for frying

For the Eger (red wine) Sauce:

1 tbsp redcurrant jelly

$^1/_4$ pint lamb gravy or stock

$^1/_4$ pint red wine or port wine

Method

To make the sauce, heat all ingredients together until the jelly has melted. Boil mushroom caps in water with salt and lemon juice until just tender. Stuff with paté and sandwich 2 caps together. Coat with eggs then breadcrumbs, then deep fry for a few minutes until lightly browned. Drain and serve immediately with red wine sauce.

STUFFED PANCAKES HORTO BAGY STYLE

Ingredients

veal stew with paprika

pancakes

cream and sour cream to taste

Method

Prepare veal stew with paprika. Mince cooked meat and use to stuff pancakes. Pile into ovenproof dish and cover with sauce made from stew gravy, cream and sour cream. Serve hot.

HUNGARIAN APPLE PIE

Ingredients

1 lb cooking apples

4 oz butter

1-2 tbsp milk

6 oz plain flour

1 egg, separated

2 oz ground almonds

strawberry jam

Method

Stew apples in as little water as possible. Sieve flour, rub in butter and mix to a dough with egg yolk and milk. Leave in cool place for 30 mins. Line 7-inch sandwich tin with half the pastry and partly blind bake for 10 mins. Mix ground almonds with sugar. Spread pastry with jam and cover with half the almond mixture. Fold stiffly whisked egg white into apple and put in pie tin. Sprinkle rest of sugar and almond mixture on top and cover with remaining pastry. Brush with milk and sprinkle with sugar. Bake in a hot oven for 25-30 mins.   Serve with cream.

Everyday Thoughts
for everyday living

"The fruits of labour are the sweetest
of all pleasures."

Luc de Vauvenargues

"Laughter has no foreign accent."

Paul Lowney

"The most wasted day is that
in which we have not laughed."

Chamfort

"Learning is ever young,
even in old age."

Aeschylus

"Learn as though you would never be
able to master it; hold it as though you
would be in fear of losing it."

Confucius

L

Name
✉

☎
Name
✉

☎
Name
✉

☎
Name
✉

☎
Name
✉

☎
Name
✉

☎

FROM SCOTLAND

SCOTCH BROTH

Ingredients

1 lb boiling beef/neck of mutton	2 carrots
4 pints water	2 leeks
2 tbsp barley (pearl)	3 tbsp swede, diced
1 tsp salt	1 onion
2 tbsp yellow split peas	$^1/_2$ small cabbage
2 tbsp dried green peas	1 dsp finely chopped parsley

Method

Put the water, salt, peas, washed pearl barley and meat into a large saucepan. Slowly bring to the boil. Skim. Dice vegetables, shred the cabbage and add. Bring back to the boil and simmer for about 2 hours until the meat is cooked and the peas tender. Add parsley, salt and pepper.

EVERYDAY SCOTCH HAGGIS

Ingredients

$^1/_2$ lb ox liver	2 pinches black pepper
4 oz shredded suet	1 teacup water
1 onion	$^3/_4$ dsp salt
4 oz oatmeal, pinhead	

Method

In a small saucepan put liver, onion and water. Boil for 15 minutes. Toast the oatmeal for a few minutes in the oven until it is light brown. Mince the liver and onion. Mix everything together with the liquid and seasoning. Serve with swedes and mashed potatoes.

PETTICOAT TAILS

Ingredients

12 oz margarine/butter	9 oz icing sugar
18 oz plain flour	1 tbsp castor sugar

Method

Cream the butter and sift in the icing sugar. Beat the flour in with the icing sugar, adding sufficient water to make a firm dough. Roll the dough out thinly into a large square. Cut it into 2-inch triangles. Place the triangles on a greased baking sheet and bake at 325°F (or equivalent temperature) for 30 minutes. Remove from oven and dust with castor sugar while they are still hot. Leave the triangles on the tray to cool.

Everyday Thoughts
for everyday living

"We make a living by what we get,
but we make a life by what we give."

Norman MacEwan

"It is not the years in your life but
the life in your years that counts!"

Adlai Stevenson

"The love we give away is the only
love we keep."

Elbert Hubbard

"Treasure the love you receive above
all. It will survive long after your gold
and good health have vanished."

Og Mandino

"Who, being loved, is poor?"

Oscar Wilde

Addresses • Addresses • Addresses • Addresses • Addresses

Name
✉

☎
Name
✉

☎
Name
✉

☎
Name
✉

☎
Name
✉

☎
Name
✉

☎

FRIENDS & FOOD PREFERENCES

Little can be so disheartening to the cook to learn that a meal that has been hours in the preparation is poison to one of the guests - maybe he or she is a vegetarian, allergic to eggs, detests olives . . . !
Avoid uncomfortable situations by keeping a record of your friends' most important food preferences.

Friend ....
Allergies/
Dislikes ....

Friend ....
Allergies/
Dislikes ....
....

Friend ....
Allergies/
Dislikes ....

Friend ....
Allergies/
Dislikes ....

Friend ....
Allergies/
Dislikes ....
....

Friend ....
Allergies/
Dislikes ....

Friend ....
Allergies/
Dislikes ....

Friend ....
Allergies/
Dislikes ....
....

Friend ....
Allergies/
Dislikes ....

Friend ....
Allergies/
Dislikes ....

Friend ....
Allergies/
Dislikes ....
....

Friend ....
Allergies/
Dislikes ....

Notes ....
....
....

Everyday Thoughts
for everyday living

"Marriage is an empty box.
It remains empty unless you put in
more than you take out."

Author Unidentified

"Married couples who love each
other tell each other a thousand
things without talking."

Chinese Proverb

"Often the difference between a successful marriage and a mediocre one
consists of leaving about three or four
things a day unsaid."

Harlan Miller

"Marriage is three parts love and seven
parts forgiveness of sins."

Langdon Mitchell

"There is no more lovely, friendly and
charming relationship, communion or
company than a good marriage."

Martin Luther

• Name
✉

☎
Name
✉

☎
Name
✉

☎
Name
✉

☎
Name
✉

☎
Name
✉

☎

DINNER PARTY RECORDS

Date/Occasion ....

Guests   Menu

....

....

....

....

....

....

Notes ....

....

....

Date/Occasion ....

Guests   Menu

....

....

....

....

....

....

....

Notes ....

....

....

Everyday Thoughts
for everyday living

"Memory is the treasury and guardian of all things."

Cicero

"God gave us memories that we might have roses in December."

James M Barrie

"The greatest mistake you can make in life is to be continually fearing you will make one."

Elbert Hubbard

"He who makes no mistakes never makes anything."

English Proverb

"The shortest mistakes are always the best."

J B Molière

M

Name

✉

☎

Name

✉

☎

Name

✉

☎

Name

✉

☎

Name

✉

☎

Name

✉

☎

DINNER PARTY RECORDS

Date/Occasion ....

Guests   Menu

....
....
....
....
....
....

Notes ....
....
....

Date/Occasion ....

Guests   Menu

....
....
....
....
....
....
....

Notes ....
....
....

Everyday Thoughts
for everyday living

"What's in a name?
That which we call a rose,
By any other name would smell as sweet."

Shakespeare: Romeo & Juliet

"A nation reveals itself not only by the
men it produces but also by the men it
honours, the men it remembers."

John F Kennedy

"Those things are better which are
perfected by nature than those which
are finished by art."

Cicero

"God made the beauties of nature
like a child playing in the sand."

Ascribed to Apollonius of Tyana

"Better is a neighbour that is near
than a brother far off."

Proverbs 27:10

Name
✉

☎
Name
✉

☎
Name
✉

☎
Name
✉

☎
Name
✉

☎
Name
✉

☎

DINNER PARTY RECORDS

Date/Occasion ....

Guests   Menu

....

....

....

....

....

....

....

Notes   ....

....

....

Date/Occasion ....

Guests   Menu

....

....

....

....

....

....

....

Notes   ....

....

....

Everyday Thoughts
for everyday living

"When your neighbour's house is afire, your own property is at stake."

Horace

"Night is the mother of counsels."

George Herbert

"The day is done, and the darkness
Falls from the wings of Night,
As a feather is wafted downward
From an eagle in his flight."

Longfellow

"Be noble! and the nobleness that lies
In other men, sleeping, but never dead,
Will rise in majesty to meet thine own."

James Russell Lowell

"How sad would be November if we had no knowledge of the spring!"

Edwin Way Teale

N

Name
✉

☎
Name
✉

☎
Name
✉

☎
Name
✉

☎
Name
✉

☎
Name
✉

☎

HANDY HINTS

ANIMAL HAIR

Use sellotape to remove animal hair from clothes, furniture etc. Simply wrap the sellotape around your fingers (sticky side outward) and rub over the hairs.

ANTS

You can discourage ants in the house by sprinkling bicarbonate of soda or powdered borax of cloves on shelves and in drawers.

ASH

Do not empty these into a wastepaper basket as they can easily start a fire. A large tin is much more suitable. To prevent cigarette ends from burning in an ashtray and to reduce the smell of stale tobacco, coat the bottom of the ashtray with baking powder.

BAKING TINS

To discourage a new baking tin from rusting, rub it inside and out with lard and place it in an oven at moderate heat for forty-five minutes. When cool wipe thoroughly with a paper towel. To remove rust from tinware rub with half a raw potato that has been dipped in scouring powder. Rinse and then dry - ideally in an oven.

BALL POINT PENS

If a ballpoint pen doesn't work try warming the point gently with a match or by pouring boiling water over it.

BARBECUE

To maximise the heat line your barbecue with tin-foil, shiny side up. Use left over brewed coffee to clean the barbecue set.

BATHS

If you have unsightly stains on your bath or wash basin due to a dripping tap, try rubbing with a paste made of lemon juice and salt and rinsing well. Failing this, try rubbing them with a toothbrush using a paste of cream of tartar and peroxide and then rinsing.

BOOKS

To keep your books in good condition do not place them tight against a wall, but leave a couple of centimetres gap to enable the air to circulate around them. Also, make sure they are kept upright and not leaning at an angle as this would be bad for their bindings.

If the pages of a book are torn slightly, place them in position and smear lightly with the white of an egg, leaving the book open to dry.

Carpet tape is useful when trying to repair the spine of a book.

BOTTLES

Stick an adhesive plaster over the cork of the bottle containing liquid when packing to help prevent accidents. It is also advisable to pack bottles between soft items.

Bottles are best emptied by shaking them in a circular motion.

Everyday Thoughts
for everyday living

"The woman who obeys her husband rules him."

Spanish Proverb

"An old man loved is winter with flowers."

German Proverb

"Our opinions are less important than the spirit and temper with which they possess us, and even good opinions are worth very little unless we hold them in a broad, intelligent, and spacious way."

John Morley

"Every man values himself more than all the rest of men, but he always values others' opinions of himself more than his own."

Marcus Aurelius

O

Name
✉

☎
Name
✉

☎
Name
✉

☎
Name
✉

☎
Name
✉

☎
Name
✉

☎

HANDY HINTS

If you find difficulty unscrewing a bottle or container give a firm tap to the bottom of the container.

Remove strong odours from bottles by filling them with a mixture of cold water and four teaspoons of dry mustard and leaving them to stand for a least half a day before rinsing well.

BREAD BOARDS

If your wooden bread board is warped, place it on a flat surface and cover it with a wet cloth, leaving it for at least 24 hours.

BROOMS

When a broom handle does not fit anymore then wrap with adhesive tape and screw the handle back into the socket. This should help keep it in place.

CANDLES

To increase the life span of candles keep them in the freezer for a few hours before use.

To make candles fit into candle sticks dip the end in hot water until it is soft enough to fit into the required size.

Wash the candle stick holder in soapy water with a few drops of ammonia to remove the wax.

CAR

To prevent bumping your car in a tight garage attach an old tyre to the wall.

To clean a very dirty car use a mixture of methy-lated spirit and water (1 unit of methylated spirit to 8 units of water). Do not rinse. This should leave your car shining.

CARPETS

When choosing a carpet ask to see it flat on the floor. The colour might look quite different when the carpet is displayed rolled vertically.

To restore the life to carpet pile which has been flattened by furniture legs, place several layers of wet cloth onto the area. Then hold a hot iron lightly on top of the cloth. The steam should bring back the bounce to the carpet which can then be fluffed up using a nail brush.

CHINA

Protect your best china plates from chips and cracks by alternating them with paper plates or corrugated paper when storing them or when packing them.

COOKING SMELLS

Get rid of unwanted cooking smells by boiling one teaspoon of ground cinnamon or ground cloves in a $\frac{1}{4}$ litre of water for fifteen minutes.

CORK

Cork expands. If it does not fit back into the bottle then place it in boiling water for a few minutes until it becomes soft. It will then fit easily back into the bottle.

CRYSTAL

To give a real sparkle to your crystal add a few drops of ammonia to the washing water and vinegar to the rinsing water.

Everyday Thoughts
for everyday living

"One often contradicts an opinion when it is really only the tone in which it has been presented that is unsympathetic."

Nietzsche

"When we stop to think, we often miss our opportunity."

Publilius Syrus

"A wise man will make more opportunities than he finds."

Francis Bacon

"An optimist sees an opportunity in every calamity: a pessimist sees a calamity in every opportunity."

Author Unidentified

"Originality does not consist in saying what no one has ever said before, but in saying exactly what you think yourself."

James Fitz-James Stephen

O

Name
✉

☎
Name
✉

☎
Name
✉

☎
Name
✉

☎
Name
✉

☎
Name
✉

☎

HANDY HINTS

DAMPNESS

To determine whether dampness is caused by condensation or is coming from outside, attach a piece of silver foil to the affected area. If moisture appears on the front surface then this is caused by condensation in the room and you should look for better ways of ventilating the room. If, however, the foil is wet on the side of the wall, the damp comes from the outside and you should seek professional help.

DECORATING

When you have decorated a room, make sure you keep a note of the number of rolls of wallpaper or tins of paint that you used, so that when you come to redecorating, you will know exactly what you need.

DISHWASHERS

Pour 4 heaped tablespoons of bicarbonate of soda through the bottom rack of your dishwasher and put it on the rinse cycle to refresh the smell.

DOORS

Silence a creaky door by rubbing soap along the hinges.

DRAWERS

If you have trouble opening tight fitting drawers, rub soap or candle wax along the upper edges to lubricate them.

DRILLING

To stop the drill from slipping when drilling a hole into metal or ceramic tiles, cover the mark with adhesive tape, drill through it and then remove the tape.

When drilling into the ceiling, drill through the base of an old squash bottle or transparent plastic container and this will catch the chips and stop them from going into your eyes.

EASTER EGGS

Use natural products to dye Easter eggs: beetroot juice will make a red dye, saffron will give you yellow, and spinach juice will produce a green colour.

EGG BOXES

Cardboard or fibre egg boxes are ideal for growing seeds. When the shoots are ready for planting, just bury the entire tray. The roots will not be disturbed and the tray will disintegrate after a while.

ELECTRIC-WIRE

When fitting a plug it is often difficult to cut the rubber which encompasses the wire without cutting the copper thread. If you warm the rubber with a match you will be able to strip it very easily with your fingers.

ENAMEL

If your enamel is cracked and the cracks become dirty, make a thick paste of French chalk and water and coat the enamel with it. Leave it until the paste dries out and begins to crack and then brush off. Repeat until the cracks come clean.

ERASERS

Washing-up liquid effectively cleans dirty erasers.

Everyday Thoughts
for everyday living

"If we live in peace ourselves,
we in turn may bring peace to others.
A peaceable man does more good than
a learned one."

Thomas À Kempis

"Perfection is attained by slow degrees; it
requires the hand of time."

Voltaire

"By perseverance the snail
reached the Ark."

C H Spurgeon

"Philosophy triumphs easily over past, and
over future evils, but present evils triumph
over philosophy."

François de la Rochefoucauld

"The entire world would perish,
if pity were not to limit anger."

Seneca the Elder

Addresses • Addresses • Addresses • Addresses • Addresses

Name
✉

☎
Name
✉

☎
Name
✉

☎
Name
✉

☎
Name
✉

☎
Name
✉

☎

FELT-TIPPED PENS

If your felt-tip pen seems to have run out, try dipping the tip in a little vinegar - this should give it a new lease of life. Store felt-tip pens tip downwards with the cap on so that they are always ready to use.

FINGER NAILS

If you want to take care of your nails, never cut them with scissors as this can cause them to split. File them with an emery board - from the sides up to the tip (and never in a see-saw movement) - as this is softer than a metal file.

FIREPLACES

If you are lighting a fire in a chimney which has not been used for some time and which may be damp, first burn a creased sheet of newspaper in the grate. This should remove the moisture from the chimney and help you get the best out of the fireplace.

When burning a fire, do not burn coloured magazines or newspaper as the coloured ink will give off some lead vapour when burning.

FLIES

A pleasant way of discouraging flies is by placing cotton wool balls sprinkled with a few drops of lavender oil on saucers around the room. Basil or mint grown in pots on the windowsill or in a window box is also a sweet smelling way of deterring flies.

FLOORS

Talcum powder sprinkled between floorboards will help to stop them from squeaking.

FLOWERS

If you are picking flowers from the garden, do not do it during the warmest part of the day as the flowers will not last long. Pick them in the

early morning or early evening if you want them to last longer.

FOIL

Wrap food tightly in kitchen foil for storing but loosely for cooking.

FRAMING

Insert kitchen foil behind the picture when framing to prevent damage from damp.

FREEZER

When you have defrosted your freezer rub the inside with glycerine. Next time you come to defrost it you should find that the ice will come away easily.

To stop packages from sticking to the freezer walls or bottom, do not put them straight back into the freezer after defrosting but leave the freezer empty for half an hour first.

Everyday Thoughts
for everyday living

"Poetry is the opening and closing of a door, leaving those who look through to guess about what is seen during a moment."

Carl Sandburg

"It is not the man who has little, but he who desires more, that is poor."

Seneca

"The sole advantage of power is that you can do more good."

Baltasar Gracián

"Prejudice is the child of ignorance."

William Hazlitt

"Problems are opportunities in work clothes."

Henry Kaiser

"To the pure all things are pure."

Titus 1:15

Addresses • Addresses • Addresses • Addresses • Addresses • Addresses

Name

✉

☎

Name

✉

☎

Name

✉

☎

Name

✉

☎

Name

✉

☎

Name

✉

☎

FURNITURE

When it is exposed to direct sunlight, polished furniture will permanently lose its veneer. To avoid lasting damage, either position the piece of furniture elsewhere, or keep it covered with a cloth.

FUSES

Keep a torch and a card of fuse wire beside the fuse box in case of an emergency.

GARDEN TOOLS

To remove rust from your garden tools use wire wool dipped in turpentine.

GARLIC

To remove the smell of garlic from your breath try chewing some fresh mint, a coffee bean, a stalk of parsley or celery or some cardamom seeds!

GIFT WRAP

When you are wrapping large numbers of presents, at Christmas for example or at a children's party, try using attractive leftover wallpaper which makes a far cheaper alternative to gift wrap.

GLASSES

If two glasses have stuck together and you are finding it difficult to separate them, stand the bottom glass in hot (not boiling) water and fill the top one with cold water. This should cause them to separate without damaging them.

To get rid of small chips around the rim of a glass, rub them with fine sandpaper until smooth.

Stand a silver spoon in a glass or jar to prevent it from cracking when boiling water is poured into it.

GLUE

Fit a piece of candle on the top of a glue bottle and use it as a stopper to close the bottle. As glue does not stick to candle wax you should no longer have any problems when you come to open it.

GRASS

To prevent grass from growing between the cracks in your paving stones or path, sprinkle salt in them, or pour on very salted boiling water.

GREENFLY

You can help to discourage greenfly by planting garlic around the plants that attract the greenfly. When the garlic starts sprouting, keep the shoots cut back.

GUTTERS

A piece of chicken wire placed over the top of your gutter will effectively prevent falling leaves from blocking it.

Everyday Thoughts
for everyday living

"Quarrels would not last long if the fault was only on one side."

François de la Rochefoucauld

"The second word makes the quarrel."

Japanese Proverb

"Most quarrels amplify a misunderstanding."

André Gide

"You can make up a quarrel but it will always show where it was patched."

Edgar Watson Howe

"Better is a handful with quietness, than both the hands full with travails and vexation of spirit."

Ecclesiastes 4:6

"No wealth is like the quiet mind."

Author Unidentified

Addresses · Addresses · Addresses · Addresses · Addresses · Addresses

Name
✉

☎
Name
✉

☎
Name
✉

☎
Name
✉

☎
Name
✉

☎
Name
✉

☎

HANDY HINTS

HANGERS

If you have a skirt without any loops and are short of special hangers, wind a rubber band around each end of an ordinary hanger to prevent the skirt from falling off, or put two clothes pegs on an ordinary wire hanger.

HARD WATER DEPOSITS

If you find hard water deposits in jugs, bottles, vases or glasses etc., fill the object with malt vinegar and leave it for a few hours or as long as necessary. Then rub off with a fine wire scouring pad and rinse thoroughly. The vinegar can be reused.

HOSE

To make the hose fit easily onto the tap rub the inside of the hose with some soap. The soap will quickly dry when the hose is fitted.

HOT-WATER BOTTLES

When filling a hot-water bottle lie it flat on its back holding the neck upright. This will prevent the water splashing due to air-bubbles in the bottle. Add a little salt to the water to keep it warm longer.

INSECTS

By hanging a fresh bunch of stinging nettles in front of any open windows or doors, you can discourage flies and wasps from invading your house.

IRONING

Starch can be removed from the bottom of your iron by sprinkling a piece of paper with some fine kitchen salt and rubbing the iron over it until the base becomes smooth again, or by rubbing the base with half a lemon dipped in fine kitchen salt.

A few drops of your favourite toilet water mixed with the water in the iron or sprinkled first on the ironing board will perfume your linen lightly.

IVORY

Very dirty ivory can be cleaned by leaving the item to soak for a few hours in milk and then washing it with warm soapy water.

To keep small pieces of ivory white, place them in the direct sunlight. Alternatively, to colour a piece of ivory which looks too new, dip it in strong tea or coffee. Do not leave it to soak but keep dipping it in and out until the desired effect is reached. Dry and polish.

Everyday Thoughts
for everyday living

"It is reason that produces everything: virtue, genius, wit, talent, and taste. What is virtue? Reason in practice. Talent? Reason enveloped in glory. Wit? Reason which is chastely expressed. Taste is nothing else than reason delicately put in force, and genius is reason in its most sublime form."

M J de Chenier

"Opportunities flit by while we sit regretting the chances we have lost, and the happiness that comes to us we heed not, because of the happiness that is gone."

Jerome K Jerome

"To regret deeply is to live afresh."

Thoreau

"Work is the price which is paid for reputation."

Baltasar Gracian

Name

✉

☎

Name

✉

☎

Name

✉

☎

Name

✉

☎

Name

✉

☎

Name

✉

☎

Addresses • Addresses • Addresses • Addresses • Addresses • Addresses

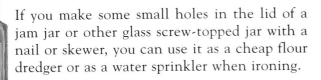

JARS

Leave a few drops of bleach in a glass jar to remove strong fish or pickle smells. You will have to leave the bleach in for at least twelve hours.

If you make some small holes in the lid of a jam jar or other glass screw-topped jar with a nail or skewer, you can use it as a cheap flour dredger or as a water sprinkler when ironing.

JAR LABELS

Do not label your jars until the contents have cooled, otherwise the labels will come unstuck.

JEWELLERY

If you want to give a quick shine to gold jewellery, rub the item with a ball of soft bread. Likewise if you want an item of silver jewellery to shine, rub it with half a lemon and then rinse before drying.

To loosen or remove a ring which is stuck on your finger, wash your hands with soap and water and try to take the ring off while the soap is still on your hands.

KETTLES

Place a marble in your kettle to prevent it from furring. To defur a kettle fill it with water and put the kettle in your freezer. When it defrosts the ice will pull the fur of the sides. Alternatively, pour in a small quantity of vinegar (enough to cover the element where applicable), bring it to the boil then agitate it. Leave it to cool and then rinse thoroughly. It may be necessary to repeat these processes several times.

KEYS

Covering a rusty key with turpentine and leaving it to soak for a couple of hours before rubbing and drying it should bring its shine back.

KNITWEAR

To prevent your knitwear from stretching when you are washing it in the washing machine, place it first inside a pillowcase.

LEATHER SHOES

When drying leather shoes or boots, never be tempted to do so quickly in front of the fire as the leather will harden and will be more likely to crack.

LIDS

If you cannot unscrew a lid, place the jar in boiling water for a few minutes. It should then become loose and easy to unscrew.

LIGHT BULBS

You can delicately scent your room by rubbing just a few drops of your favourite perfume onto a light bulb. A pleasant smell will be emitted when the light bulb is on.

LINEN

To prevent fine linen which is not in constant use from becoming discoloured and yellow, wrap it in blue tissue paper.

LINOLEUM

Unsightly black marks on linoleum floors can be removed quite simply by using a pencil-eraser. A few drops of paraffin in the water when washing will help make linoleum shine.

Everyday Thoughts
for everyday living

"Respect a man, he will do the more."

James Howell

"If you have some respect for people as they are, you can be more effective in helping them to become better than they are."

John W Gardner

"He that can take rest is greater than he that can take cities."

Benjamin Franklin

"It is better to be miserable and rich than it is to be miserable and poor."

Author Unidentified

"The rich man is not one who is in possession of much, but one who gives much."

St. John Chrysostom

Addresses • Addresses • Addresses • Addresses • Addresses

Name
✉

☎
Name
✉

☎
Name
✉

☎
Name
✉

☎
Name
✉

☎
Name
✉

☎

LIPSTICK

When you are testing a lipstick for colour, the best place to try it is on the cushion of your finger, where the skin is pinkish, like the lips.

LOCKS

When you cannot get your key to turn in a lock and it seems to be jammed, rub the key with vaseline, or, failing that, butter or margarine. This should help to ease the lock.

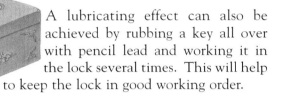

A lubricating effect can also be achieved by rubbing a key all over with pencil lead and working it in the lock several times. This will help to keep the lock in good working order.

MATS

You can help to prevent the edges of a mat from curling up by pasting some very thick starch along the edge and then ironing over some brown paper with a fairly hot iron.

MATCHES

A damp match can be made to light by coating the tip in nail varnish. You do not even have to wait for the nail varnish to dry before striking it. An alternative is to rub it against the bristles of a brush.

MICROWAVE OVENS

You can help to remove stubborn and unpleasant cooking smells from inside a microwave oven by placing a teacup containing 3 parts water to 1 part lemon juice or vinegar inside it and cooking for eight to ten minutes on the lowest setting. Wipe the oven dry afterwards.

MIRRORS

If, before you run your bath, you rub the bathroom mirror with a few drops of shampoo, this will help prevent it from steaming up.

MOTHS

Small muslin bags filled with aromatic plants placed in your wardrobe and drawers will deter moths and will make your clothes smell nice at the same time.

NAILS

When hammering small nails use a hairslide as a holder or stick plasticine over the area you wish to hammer the nail into. This will hold the nail in position and will protect your fingers.

To prevent cracking the plaster when hammering in nails, first stick a piece of sellotape or masking tape to the wall, then hammer the nail in through the tape.

When trying to remove a nail which has been painted over, first soften the paint by holding a lighted match just below it, being careful not to burn the wall.

NAIL VARNISH

You can keep the top of a bottle of nail varnish from sticking and becoming difficult to open by spreading a little vaseline on the grooves.

Storing the bottle in the fridge will prevent the nail varnish from getting a sticky consistency and it will also help the varnish to last longer. If the varnish thickens, it can be brought back to a better consistency by adding just a few drops of nail varnish remover.

Everyday Thoughts
for everyday living

"Silence is as full of potential wisdom and wit as the unhewn marble of great sculpture."

Aldous Huxley

"The art of art, the glory of expression and the sunshine of the light of letters, is simplicity."

Walt Whitman

"Sincerity is the highest compliment you can pay."

Ralph Waldo Emerson

"Sorrow is better than fear . . . Fear is a journey, a terrible journey, but sorrow is at least an arriving."

Alan Paton: Cry the Beloved Country

"Our joys as winged dreams do fly, Why then should sorrow last?"

Thomas Percy

Addresses • Addresses • Addresses • Addresses • Addresses • Addresses

Name
✉

☎
Name
✉

☎
Name
✉

☎
Name
✉

☎
Name
✉

☎
Name
✉

☎

NEWSPAPER

Roll a newspaper into a long thin tube, knotted in the middle, when you are lighting a fire.

OVENS

Next time you clean your oven, after cleaning and drying it rub it all over with a paste made of bicarbonate of soda and water. This should make it easier to wipe clean next time around.

PAINT

When selecting a single colour for the walls of a room, always choose one a shade lighter than you want, as paint tends to look darker once it is on the wall.

To keep the top of a paint tin clean, when painting place a paper plate over the top of the tin with the middle cut out. This way all the drops will land on the plate and not on the tin, and the plate can simply be discarded after you have finished painting.

The strong smell left in your house after you have been painting can be avoided by using a mixture of one tablespoon of vanilla essence to two pints paint when you are painting. Or while painting, try adding a couple of tablespoons of ammonia to one or two shallow containers of water placed in the room you are working on - this should stop the smell from spreading around the house.

PAINTBRUSHES

Dried out brushes can be restored to life by immersing them in hot vinegar, while errant bristles can be encouraged to return to their proper place by spraying the brush head with hairspray, smoothing and leaving to dry.

PAINT TUBES

To get a stubborn cap off a small tube of artist's paint, try holding a lighted match under the cap for just a few seconds.

PAN

Before using a new pan, boil some vinegar in it for a few minutes to prevent food from sticking.

PARCELS

When you are wrapping a parcel using string, first dip the string in warm water and then tie the knot. When the string dries it will shrink, leaving you with a tight knot.

PIANOS

Do not place a lot of books or ornaments on the top of a piano as it will deaden the tone. If a piano key stays down when it is struck then it is a sign of dampness.

Everyday Thoughts
for everyday living

"It is excellent
To have a giant's strength,
but it is tyrannous
To use it like a giant."

Shakespeare: Measure for Measure

"The true measure of success is not what
you have, but what you can do without."

Author Unidentified

"He has achieved success who has lived
well, laughed often and loved much."

Bessie Anderson Stanley

"Know how sublime a thing it is to
suffer and be strong."

Longfellow

"Pity may represent little more than the
impersonal concern which prompts the
mailing of a cheque, but true sympathy is
the personal concern which demands the
giving of one's soul."

Martin Luther King

S

Name
✉

☎
Name
✉

☎
Name
✉

☎
Name
✉

☎
Name
✉

☎
Name
✉

☎

Ivory keys will become yellowed more quickly if the lid of the piano is kept down, as ivory yellows more in the dark.

PINS

If you keep a small magnet in your pin box, then if you drop it the keys will be more likely to cluster around the magnet, making it easier to collect them.

PLASTIC BOTTLES

For easier and more compact disposal of your plastic bottles, pour a small quantity of boiling water into the bottle. This will cause it to become soft and to collapse, making it easier to crush the bottle in your hands.

PLASTICINE

A quick substitute for plasticine for children to play with can be made by making a dough with flour, water and salt. This can be coloured with a little paprika or mustard powder to make it more attractive, and it will stay soft if stored in a sealed plastic bag.

If you do not want to use a trellis and yet still wish your ivy to grow up the wall, encourage it by sticking it to the wall from time to time with plasticine.

PLASTERS

If you find removing sticking plaster from your skin painful, first rub baby oil over the plaster. You should find it easier to remove.

REFRIGERATORS

A piece of charcoal placed inside your fridge will absorb the smells of strong food such as fish and cheese and will only need to be replaced every five-to-six months.

If your fridge is noisy it could simply be that it is not standing on a level surface.

RUBBER GLOVES

As hands sweat a lot in rubber gloves, they may become damp and smell unpleasant. Avoid this by dusting the inside of the gloves with talc when you use them and by washing the insides from time to time. It will also help if you dry the gloves inside out after you have used them.

RUBBISH

To keep dogs and cats away from your rubbish sprinkle pure ammonia over the bags.

RUGS

To keep a rug from slipping or wrinkling on a carpet or shiny floor, stick some plastic stick-ons, commonly used for the bath, on the underside of the rug. Alternatively, you could sew or glue pieces of carpet, pile downwards, under the corners of the rug.

RUST

Rust on utensils can be removed by rubbing the stains with a cork dipped in olive oil. Rust stains on metal will sometimes disappear when rubbed with half a raw onion.

SCISSORS

To sharpen your scissors cut a sheet of emery paper into small pieces.

Everyday Thoughts
for everyday living

"Waste not fresh tears over old griefs."

Euripides

"There's no seeing one's way through tears."

English Proverb

"Why comes temptation
but for man to meet
And master and make crouch
beneath his foot,
And so be pedestalled in triumph?"

Robert Browning

"I can resist everything except
temptation."

Oscar Wilde: Lady Windermere's Fan

"Our life is what our thoughts make it."

Marcus Aurelius

T

Name
✉

☎
Name
✉

☎
Name
✉

☎
Name
✉

☎
Name
✉

☎
Name
✉

☎

SHINE

Black or dark coloured clothes often become shiny with wear. This can be alleviated by brushing the shiny part with black coffee - half a teacup of strong black coffee to half a teacup of water. Then press with a cloth. Alternatively, you could rub the article with a piece of clean cloth dampened with turpentine or white spirit. The smell will soon disappear.

SHOES

When buying shoes, wait until the afternoon. Your feet tend to be relaxed first thing in the morning after a night's sleep but may swell slightly during the day, so if you buy your shoes early in the morning you may find that they pinch you in the evening.

Remove the odour from smelly shoes by sprinkling a tablespoon of bicarbonate of soda inside each shoe and leaving it overnight.

When drying wet shoes, stuff them with newspaper to help them keep their shape.

SHOWER CURTAINS

To prevent mildew on your cloth shower curtains, soak them for half an hour in a strong solution of salted water, then hang them up to dry. Rubbing the curtains with bicarbonate of soda will also help remove mildew.

SLUGS

One of the less offensive ways of killing slugs is by distributing bran around the garden, which they are attracted to but which kills them. (The bran will also attract snails, who will assemble around it making it easy to collect them).

Alternatively, you can entice the slugs with a glass of beer left in the garden overnight.

SMOKE

To prevent a room from be-coming smoky when people are smoking in it, try lighting a few candles, or strategically arrange a few small containers filled with vinegar. This should help to eliminate the smoke from the room.

STAINS

When removing a stain, work from the edge of the stain inwards. This will help prevent the stain from spreading.

STAMPS

When you wish to remove an unused stamp from an envelope without damaging it, submerge the corner of the envelope with the stamp on it in boiling water for a few minutes. The stamp should then come off easily and can be left to dry.

Another method is to wet the back of the stamp inside the envelope with lighter fluid.

STICKY LABELS

Stubborn sticky labels on glass or china can be removed with nail-varnish remover, cooking oil, turpentine or white spirit.

Handle negatives by the edges to avoid scratching and fingerprints which will ruin any prints made from them.

Everyday Thoughts
for everyday living

"Human thought, like God, makes the world in its own image."

Adam Clayton Powell

"Nimble thought can jump both sea and land."

Shakespeare: Sonnets

"Tolerance implies no lack of commitment to one's own beliefs. Rather it condemns the oppression of persecution of others."

John F Kennedy

"The heaviest baggage for a traveller is an empty purse."

English Proverb

"In travelling: a man must carry knowledge with him, if he would bring home knowledge."

Samuel Johnson

Name

✉

☎

Name

✉

☎

Name

✉

☎

Name

✉

☎

Name

✉

☎

Name

✉

☎

HANDY HINTS

THERMOS FLASKS

To clean a stained thermos flask put three tablespoons of bicarbonate of soda into it and fill up with warm water. Agitate it and leave to stand for quarter of an hour. Then rinse and leave to dry.

Stubborn coffee smells and stains can be eliminated by pouring in a cup of boiling water and one tablespoon of raw rice. Shake the flask for a few minutes and then rinse.

If you will not be using your flask for a while, pop a couple of lumps of sugar into it to prevent mouldy smells developing.

THREAD

To prevent your double thread tangling when sewing, knot the ends separately instead of together.

TOILET BOWLS

You can easily remove hard water marks inside the toilet bowl by pouring three teacups of vinegar into the bowl and allowing it to soak for a few hours before brushing and flushing.

VACUUM FLASK

When storing a vacuum flask empty, leave the top off to avoid getting a musty smell. If the flask does smell musty, fill it with a mixture of warm water and two tablespoons of white vinegar, leaving it to stand for several minutes before shaking and rinsing well. If this fails to eliminate the smell, try a mixture of hot water and one and a half tablespoons of bicarbonate of soda. Leave it for at least four hours and rinse well.

WALLPAPER

When storing rolls of wallpaper, keep them horizontal, not upright as the ends are more likely to get damaged if they are left standing up.

WASHING

To prevent dark clothes from picking up fluff when washed with other items, turn inside out before placing them in the washing machine.

WASHING-UP LIQUID BOTTLE

A clean washing-up liquid bottle filled with water is an ideal watering can for your house plants, enabling you to control the water and to avoid spillages.

WASTE-DISPOSAL UNIT

To clean your waste disposal unit, sprinkle a dozen or so ice cubes with scouring powder and pass them through it, finishing with a few orange or lemon peels.

WATCHES

If the glass of your watch gets misted up, turn it over and wear the glass next to your skin for a little while. The warmth from your skin will help to clear the mist.

WATERING PLANTS

If you are going away on holiday and can find no one to water your plants, keep them moist by soaking the soil thoroughly and then placing the plant and pot, still dripping, in a polythene bag. Close the bag tightly and place in a position where the plant will receive indirect sunlight.

Everyday Thoughts
for everyday living

"Uncertainty is the worst of all evils until the moment when reality makes us regret uncertainty."

Alphonse Karr

"All uncertainty is fruitful . . . so long as it is accompanied by the wish to understand."

Antonio Machado

"Understanding is the beginning of approving."

André Gide

"In what we really understand we reason but little."

William Hazlitt

"Between our birth and death we may touch understanding as a moth brushes a window with its wing."

Christopher Fry

Name
✉

☎
Name
✉

☎
Name
✉

☎
Name
✉

☎
Name
✉

☎
Name
✉

☎

Addresses · Addresses · Addresses · Addresses · Addresses · Addresses

HANDY HINTS

WEIGHT

When you are keeping an eye on your weight, weigh yourself at the same time of the day once a week. This will give you a truer idea of any weight loss or gain by counteracting any daily fluctuations.

WINDOWS

When painting window frames, protect the glass from paint by laying strips of dampened newspaper along the edges and in the corners. These will be easy to remove afterwards.

WOOL

Thick wool can be difficult to thread - if you damp it with saliva it tends to just bounce back. Instead, try rolling the tip on a wet piece of soap and then rub it between your fingers. The ply should then stick together.

WRINKLES IN CLOTHES

If you do not have access to an iron, for example if you are travelling, hang the clothes in the bathroom and fill the bath with hot water. If you close the door and leave for a while, the steam should help remove the creases from your garments.

ZIPS

A zip can be helped to run smoothly by rubbing it with a little soft soap, some candle wax or a pencil lead.

Everyday Thoughts
for everyday living

"To understand all is to pardon all."
[Tout comprendre rend très indulgent.]

Anna Louise de Stael

"A man should always consider how much
he has more than he wants,
and how much more unhappy he
might be than he really is."

Joseph Addison

"When spiders' webs unite,
they can tie up a lion."

Ethiopian Proverb

"Not vain the weakest,
if their force unite."

Homer

"Once men are caught up in an event they
cease to be afraid. Only the unknown
frightens men."

Saint-Exupéry

U

Name
✉

☎
Name
✉

☎
Name
✉

☎
Name
✉

☎
Name
✉

☎
Name
✉

☎

Wine Records

Label   --

Vintage   --

Grape Variety   --

Country   --

Notes   --

Label   --

Vintage   --

Grape Variety   --

Country   --

Notes   --

Wine Records

Label

Vintage

Grape Variety

Country

Notes

Label

Vintage

Grape Variety

Country

Notes

Wine Records

Label   ....

Vintage   ....

Grape Variety   ....

Country   ....

Notes   ....

....

....

Label   ....

Vintage   ....

Grape Variety   ....

Country   ....

Notes   ....

....

Wine Records

Label

Vintage

Grape Variety

Country

Notes

Label

Vintage

Grape Variety

Country

Notes

Wine Records

Label   --

Vintage   --

Grape Variety   --

Country   --

Notes   --

Label   --

Vintage   --

Grape Variety   --

Country   --

Notes   --

Wine Records

Label

Vintage ....

Grape Variety ....

Country ....

Notes ....

....

....

....

Label ....

Vintage ....

Grape Variety ....

Country ....

Notes ....

....

Wine Records

Label ....

Vintage ....

Grape Variety ....

Country ....

Notes ....

....

....

Label ....

Vintage ....

Grape Variety ....

Country ....

Notes ....

....

Wine Records

Label

Vintage

Grape Variety

Country

Notes

Label

Vintage

Grape Variety

Country

Notes

Wine Records

Label   ---

Vintage   ---

Grape Variety   ---

Country   ---

Notes   ---

Label   ---

Vintage   ---

Grape Variety   ---

Country   ---

Notes   ---

Wine Records

Label

Vintage ....

Grape Variety ....

Country ....

Notes ....

....

....

Label ....

Vintage ....

Grape Variety ....

Country ....

Notes ....

....

Wine Labels

Wine Labels

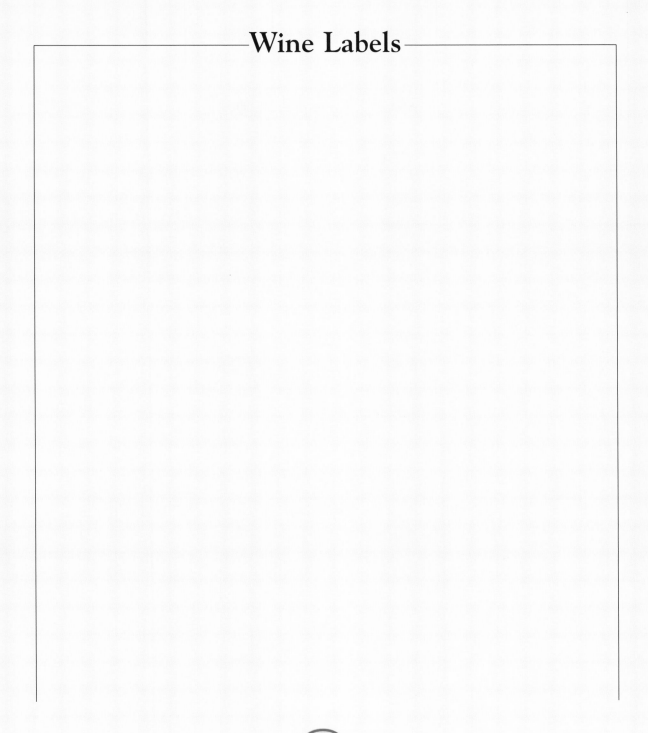

Wine Labels

Wine Labels

USEFUL INFORMATION

TEMPERATURE

F'heit	22°F	32°F	41°F	59°F	68°F	86°F
Celsius	-5°C	0°C	5°C	15°C	20°C	30°C

Conversion Formulae

$$C = \frac{5}{9} (F - 32)$$
$$F = \frac{9}{5} (C + 32)$$

ROMAN NUMERALS

I	=	1	XVI	=	16
II	=	2	XVII	=	17
III	=	3	XVIII	=	18
IV	=	4	XIX	=	19
V	=	5	XX	=	20
VI	=	6	XXX	=	30
VII	=	7	XL	=	40
VIII	=	8	L	=	50
IX	=	9	LX	=	60
X	=	10	LXX	=	70
XI	=	11	LXXX	=	80
XII	=	12	XC	=	90
XIII	=	13	C	=	100
XIV	=	14	D	=	500
XV	=	15	M	=	1000

WIND SPEEDS

1	7 mph	light wind
2	11 mph	light breeze
3	16 mph	gentle breeze
4	20 mph	moderate breeze
5	25 mph	fresh breeze
6	30 mph	strong breeze
7	35 mph	moderate gale
8	45 mph	fresh gale
9	50 mph	strong gale
10	60 mph	whole gale
11	70 mph	storm
12	80 mph	hurricane

~ INTERNATIONAL PAPER SIZES (A SERIES) ~

SIZE	MILIMETRES			INCHES		
A0	841	x	1189	33.1	x	46.8
A1	594	x	841	23.4	x	33.1
A2	420	x	594	16.5	x	23.4
A3	297	x	420	11.7	x	16.5
A4	210	x	297	8.3	x	11.7
A5	148	x	210	5.8	x	8.3
A6	105	x	148	4.1	x	5.8
A7	74	x	105	2.9	x	4.1

Everyday Thoughts
for everyday living

"It's not hard to make decisions when you know what your values are."

Roy Disney

"There are no grades of vanity, there are only grades of ability in concealing it."

Mark Twain

"The object of a good general is not to fight, but to win. He has fought enough if he gains a victory."

The Duke of Alva

"Virtue is never left to stand alone. He who has it will have neighbours."

Confucius

"Virtue is the roughest way, But proves at night a bed of down."

Sir Henry Wotton

Name

✉

☎

Name

✉

☎

Name

✉

☎

Name

✉

☎

Name

✉

☎

Name

✉

☎

USEFUL INFORMATION

~ METRIC CONVERSIONS ~

Metric Conversions	multiply by	Metric Conversions	multiply by
acres to hectares	0.4047	ounces to grammes	28.35
cubic inches to cubic centimetres	16.39	pounds to kilogrammes	0.4536
cubic feet to cubic metres	0.02832	pounds to grammes	453.6
cubic yards to cubic metres	0.7646	square inches to square centimetres	6.452
cubic inches to litres	0.01639	square feet to square metres	0.0929
feet to metres	0.3048	square yards to square metres	0.8361
gallons to litres	4.546	square miles to square kilometres	2.590
grains to grammes	0.0648	tons to kilogrammes	1016.00
inches to centimetres	2.540	yards to metres	0.9144
miles to kilometres	1.609		

~ CLOTHING SIZES ~

MEN'S SUITS & OVERCOATS

American	36	38	40	42	44	46
British	36	38	40	42	44	46
European	46	48	51	54	56	59

MEN'S SHOES

American	7½	8	8½	9½	10½	11½
British	7	7½	8	9	10	11
European	40½	41	42	43	44½	46

WOMEN'S SUITS & DRESSES

American	8	10	12	14	16	18
British	10	12	14	16	18	20
European	38	40	42	44	46	48

WOMEN'S SHOES

American	6	6½	7	7½	8	8½
British	4½	5	5½	6	6½	7
European	37½	38	39	39½	40	40½

SHIRTS

American	14	14½	15	15½	16	16½	17
British	14	14½	15	15½	16	16½	17
European	36	37	38	39	41	42	43

CHILDREN'S CLOTHES

American	4	6	8	10	12	14
British [Height (in)]	43	48	55	58	60	62
European [Height (in)]	109	122	140	147	152	157

Note: Size equivalents are approximate.

Everyday Thoughts
for everyday living

"Mankind must put an end to war or war will put an end to mankind."

John F Kennedy

"There never was a good war or a bad peace."

Benjamin Franklin

"Wealthy people miss one of life's great thrills - making the last car payment."

Author Unidentified

"You are as welcome as the flowers in May."

Charles Macklin

"The wisest man sometimes acts weakly, and the weakest sometimes wisely."

Lord Chesterfield

"Wisdom is always an overmatch for strength."

Phaedrus

Addresses • Addresses • Addresses • Addresses • Addresses

Name
✉

☎
Name
✉

☎
Name
✉

☎
Name
✉

☎
Name
✉

☎
Name
✉

☎

WEIGHTS AND MEASURES

Length

1 centimetre (cm)	=	0.3937 in		
1 metre (m)	=	100 cm	=	1.0936 yds
1 kilometre (km)	=	1000 m	=	0,6214 mile
1 inch	=	2.5400 cm		
1 yard	=	36 in	=	0.9144 m
1 mile	=	1760 yds	=	1.6093 km

Area

1 sq metre (m²)	=	10 000 cm²	=	1.1960 sq yds
1 hectare (ha)	=	10 000 m²	=	2.4711 acres
1 sq km (km²)	=	100 hectares	=	0.3861 sq mile
1 sq yd	=	9 sq ft	=	0.8361 m²
1 acre	=	4840 sq yds	=	4046.9 m²

Capacity

1 cu dm (dm³)	=	1000 cm³	=	0.0353 cu ft
1 cu metre (m³)	=	1000 dm³	=	1.3080 cu yds
1 litre	=	1dm²	=	0.2200 gallon
1 cu yd	=	27 cu ft	=	0.7646 m³
1 pint	=	4 gills	=	0.5683 litre
1 gallon	=	8 pints	=	4.5461 litres

Weight

1 gramme (g)	=	1000 mg	=	0.3535 oz
1 kilogramme (kg)	=	1000 g	=	2.2046 lb
1 tonne (t)	=	1000 kg	=	0.9842 ton
1 ounce	=	437.5 grains	=	28.350 g
1 pound	=	16 oz	=	0.4536 kg
1 ton	=	2240 pounds	=	1.0161 tonnes

Everyday Thoughts
for everyday living

"The seat of knowledge is in the head; of wisdom, in the heart.
We are sure to judge wrong if we do not feel right."

William Hazlitt

"It is easier to be wise on behalf of others than to be so for ourselves."

La Rochefoucauld

"The growth of wisdom may be gauged exactly by the dimunition of ill-temper."

Nietzsche

"I never did anything worth doing by accident, nor did any of my inventions come by accident; they came by work."

Thomas A Edison

"The biggest mistake you can make is to believe that you work for someone else."

Author Unidentified

Addresses • Addresses • Addresses • Addresses • Addresses

Name

✉

☎ Name

✉

☎ Name

✉

☎ Name

✉

☎ Name

✉

☎ Name

✉

☎

EMERGENCIES

GAS
IF YOU SMELL GAS
- Put out cigarettes. Do not use matches or naked flames.
- Do not operate electrical switches—either on or off.
- Open doors and windows to let the gas escape.
- Check to see if a tap has been left on accidentally or if a pilot light has gone out.
- If not, there is probably a gas leak. So turn off the whole supply at the meter and call gas service.

ELECTRICITY
POWER CUTS
Make things easier for yourself by planning for power cuts. Keep a good supply of candles, matches, torches and lamps (and fuel) in a place where you can find them easily in the dark. You might consider buying a calor gas or paraffin heater and/or a calor gas camping stove for such instances.

- Switch off lights and electrical appliances such as blankets, fires and cookers as they could cause an accident when the power is switched back on.
- Leave the fridge and freezer switched on, but check that the fridge drip tray is in position and keep the door closed. The freezer contents should remain unharmed for at least 8 hours but it might be an idea to insure your freezer contents anyway.
- Never let children carry candles unless accompanied by an adult. Give them a torch instead.
- When the power is restored remember to extinguish all candles.
- Reset all electric clocks including those which control central heating.

FIRE
WHAT TO DO IF FIRE BREAKS OUT
Remember that smoke can kill as well as flames. If there is smoke, or whenever the fire is too big to tackle quickly and safely:
- Get everyone out of the house at once
- Shut all doors behind you
- Call the Fire Service

If you are trapped in a room
- Keep the door shut.
- Put a blanket or carpet at the bottom of the door.
- Go to the window and call for help.

If you have to escape
- Throw a mattress out of the window and lower yourself out of the window, feet first. Hold on to the sill with your hands and drop onto the mattress.

CHIP PAN FIRES
- Switch off the heat.
- Smother the pan with a large lid or damp cloth.
- Don't move the pan or throw water on it.

ELECTRICAL FIRES
- Switch off at the socket and unplug.
- Never use water while the power is on.
- Use a dry powder extinguisher to put out the fire.

FLOODING
NATURAL DISASTER
Emergency services automatically move into operation when an area is flooded or likely to flood through adverse weather or other natural conditions. Switch off your electricity supply at the mains if it is accessible (make sure your hands are dry), if possible move on to an upper floor and wait for help to arrive.

Everyday Thoughts
for everyday living

"Our youth we can have but to-day,
We may always find time to grow old."

George Berkeley

"Youth is a fire, and the years are a
pack of wolves who grow bolder as
the fire dies down."

Author Unidentified

"It is better to waste one's youth than
to do nothing with it at all."

Georges Courteline

"Experience shows that success is due less to
ability than to zeal. The winner is he who
gives himself to his work, body and soul."

Charles Buxton

"Zeal will do more than knowledge."

William Hazlitt

Name
✉
☎
Name
✉
☎
Name
✉
☎
Name
✉
☎
Name
✉
☎
Name
✉
☎

FIRST AID

The following details are provided by St. John Ambulance. For a thorough knowledge of first aid, look out for courses held by St. John Ambulance, the British Red Cross and St. Andrew's Ambulance Association.

THE ABC OF RESUSCITATION

A *Open the Airway*

Lift the casualty's jaw and tilt his head to open the airway. Carefully remove any obvious debris from inside his mouth.

B *Check Breathing*

Look to see if his chest is rising and falling. Listen and feel for breath against your cheek.

C *Circulation – Check the Pulse*

Find the pulse in his neck by placing your fingers to the side of his voicebox and pressing gently down.

If pulse and breathing are both present . . .

Turn the casualty into the recovery position.

If there is a pulse but no breathing . . .

Start artificial ventilation. If you must leave him to send for an ambulance, give 10 breaths before going and return quickly to continue.

If there is no pulse and no breathing . . .

Phone for an ambulance, then start chest compressions combined with ventilations.

EMERGENCY AID *

Artificial Ventilation

Pinch casualty's nose firmly.

Take a deep breath and seal your lips around casualty's lips then blow into his mouth watching his chest rise. Let his chest fall completely.

Continue at about 10 breaths a minute, checking the pulse after every 10 breaths.

When breathing starts, turn him into the recovery position.

Chest Compression

Give 2 breaths of artificial ventilation. Place the heel of your hand 2 fingers breadth above the junction of rib margin and breastbone. Place your other hand on top and interlock fingers. Keeping your arms straight press down 4-5 cm (1½-2"), 15 times at a rate of 80 per minute. Repeat cycle (2 breaths to 15 compressions). If condition improves, check the pulse.

RECOVERY POSITION

Turn the casualty onto his side. Keep his head tilted with his jaw forward to maintain the open airway. Check that he cannot roll forwards or backwards. Check his breathing and pulse frequently. If they stop follow the ABC of resuscitation.

CHOKING

A foreign object sticking at the back of the throat may block the throat or induce muscular spasm.

Look out for:

Difficulty in breathing and speaking; blueness of the skin; signs from the casualty – pointing to the throat, or grasping the neck

* Never practice on healthy people.

118

JANUARY PLANNER

1
2
3
4
5
6
7
8
9
10
11
12
13
14
15
16
17
18
19
20
21
22
23
24
25
26
27
28
29
30
31

FEBRUARY PLANNER

1
2
3
4
5
6
7
8
9
10
11
12
13
14
15
16
17
18
19
20
21
22
23
24
25
26
27
28
29

FIRST AID

Your aim is:

To remove the obstruction and restore normal breathing

For an Adult

1. Bend the casualty well forwards and give five sharp slaps between the shoulder blades.

2. If this fails, try abdominal thrusts. The obstruction may be expelled by the sudden pull against the diaphragm.

3. Continue with back slaps and abdominal thrusts alternately.

4. If the casualty becomes unconscious, lay him face down upon the floor. Kneel astride him and perform abdominal thrusts.

If breathing returns, place the patient in the re-covery position and call for an ambulance. If it does not, dial 999 for an ambulance and begin resuscitation.

For a Casualty who Becomes Unconscious

1. Loss of consciousness may relieve muscle spasm, so check first to see if the casualty can now breath. If not, turn him on his side and give 4-5 blows beneath his shoulderblades.

2. If back blows fail, kneel astride the casualty and perform abdominal thrusts.

If he starts to breathe normally, place in the recovery position and call an ambulance. Check and record breathing and pulse rate every 10 minutes.

If he does not start to breathe again, dial 999 for an ambulance and begin resuscitation.

FAINTING

A faint may be a reaction to pain or fright, of the result of emotional upset, exhaustion, or lack of food. It is most common after long periods of phys ical inactivity, especially in warm atmospheres. Blood pools in the lower part of the body, reducing the amount available to the brain. Recovery from fainting is usually rapid and complete.

Look out for:

A brief loss of consciousness, a slow pulse and pallor

Your aim is:

To improve blood flow to the brain; to reassure the casualty as he recovers, and to make him comfortable

1. Lay the casualty down, and raise and support his legs.

2. Make sure he has plenty of fresh air: open a window if necessary.

3. As he recovers, reassure him and help him sit up gradually.

4. Look for and treat any injury sustained through falling.

If he does not regain consciousness quickly, check breathing and pulse, and be prepared to resuscitate if necessary. Place in the recovery position and call for an ambulance. If he starts to feel faint again, place his head between his knees and tell him to take deep breaths.

MARCH PLANNER

1
2
3
4
5
6
7
8
9
10
11
12
13
14
15
16
17
18
19
20
21
22
23
24
25
26
27
28
29
30
31

APRIL PLANNER

1
2
3
4
5
6
7
8
9
10
11
12
13
14
15
16
17
18
19
20
21
22
23
24
25
26
27
28
29
30

FIRST AID

FOREIGN BODIES IN THE SKIN

Your aim is:

To remove the splinter if it protrudes from the skin and to minimise the risk of infection

1. Clean the area around the splinter with soap and warm water. Sterilize a pair of tweezers by passing them through a flame.

2. Grasp the splinter as close to the skin as possible, and draw it out along the tract of its entry.

3. Squeeze the wound to encourage a little bleeding. Clean the area and apply an adhesive dressing. If the splinter does not come out easily or breaks up, treat as an embedded foreign body. Never probe the area (for example, with a needle).

4. Check that the casualty's tetanus immunisation is up to date. If in doubt, advise the casualty to see his doctor.

FOREIGN BODIES IN THE EYE

Look out for:

Blurred vision, pain, or discomfort; redness and watering of the eye; eyelids screwed up in spasm

Your aim is:

To prevent injury to the eye

Do not touch anything sticking to, or embedded in the eyeball, or on the coloured part of the eye. Cover the affected eye with an eye pad, bandage both eyes, then take or send the casualty to hospital.

If the object is on the white of the eye, and not stuck:

1. Advise the casualty not to rub his eye. Sit him down facing the light.

2. Gently separate the eyelids with your finger and thumb. Examine every part of his eye.

3. If you can see the foreign body, wash it out using a glass or an eye irrigator, and clean water (sterile, if possible).

4. If this is unsuccessful then, providing the foreign body is not stuck in place, lift it off with a moist swab, or the damp corner of a tissue or clean handkerchief.

If the object is under the eyelid, grasping the lashes, pull the upper lid over the lower lid. Blinking the eye under water may also make the object float clear.

FOREIGN BODIES IN THE NOSE

Look out for:

Difficulty in breathing, or noisy breathing, through the nose; swelling of the nose; smelly or blood-stained discharge indicating an object present for some time

Your aim is:

To obtain medical attention

Do not attempt to remove the foreign body – you may cause injury

1. Keep the casualty quiet. Advise him to breathe through the mouth.

2. Take or send the casualty to hospital.

FOREIGN BODIES IN THE EAR

Your aim is:

To prevent injury to the ear and to obtain medical aid if necessary

For a lodged foreign body

Do not attempt to remove the object. You may cause serious injury or push the object in further.

Take or send the casualty to hospital. Reassure him during transport or until help arrives.

MAY PLANNER

1
2
3
4
5
6
7
8
9
10
11
12
13
14
15
16
17
18
19
20
21
22
23
24
25
26
27
28
29
30
31

JUNE PLANNER

1
2
3
4
5
6
7
8
9
10
11
12
13
14
15
16
17
18
19
20
21
22
23
24
25
26
27
28
29
30

FIRST AID

For an insect in the ear

1. Sit the casualty down.
2. Gently flood the ear with tepid water so that the insect floats out.
3. If this is unsuccessful, take or send the casualty to hospital.

HOUSEHOLD POISONS

Almost every household contains poisonous substances, such as bleach, paint stripper, glue, paraffin, and weedkiller, which can be spilled, causing chemical burns, or swallowed. Children in particular are at risk from accidental household poisoning.

Preventing Poisoning in the Home

✚ Keep dangerous chemicals out of children's reach (not under the sink)

✚ Keep medicines in a locked cupboard

✚ Leave poisonous household substances in their original containers

✚ Buy medicines and household substances in tamper-proof containers

Your aim is:

To maintain airway, breathing, and circulation; to obtain medical aid; and to identify the poison

For Chemicals on the Skin

1. Wash away any residual chemical on the skin with plenty of water.

   Do not contaminate yourself with the dangerous chemical or the rinsing water.

2. Use your judgement to call a doctor or dial 999 for an ambulance. Give information about the spilled chemical.

For Swallowed Poisons

1. Check and, if necessary, clear the airway.

   If the casualty is unconscious, check breathing and pulse, and be prepared to resuscitate. If artificial ventilation is necessary, a plastic face shield will protect you if there is burning around the mouth. Place the casualty in the recovery position: he may well vomit.

   Do not try to induce vomiting.

2. Use your judgement to call a doctor or dial 999 for an ambulance. Give information about the swallowed poison.

If a conscious casualty's lips are burned by corrosive substances, give him frequent sips of cold water or milk.

INSECT STINGS

✚ If the sting is visible, gently remove with tweezers.

✚ Apply a cold pad, surgical spirit or a solution of bicarbonate of soda.

JULY PLANNER

1
2
3
4
5
6
7
8
9
10
11
12
13
14
15
16
17
18
19
20
21
22
23
24
25
26
27
28
29
30
31

AUGUST PLANNER

1
2
3
4
5
6
7
8
9
10
11
12
13
14
15
16
17
18
19
20
21
22
23
24
25
26
27
28
29
30

CHILDHOOD INFECTIONS

	MEASLES	WHOOPING COUGH	MUMPS	CHICKENPOX	GERMAN MEASLES (Rubella)	GASTRO-ENTERI-TIS
INCUBATION PERIOD	8 to 10 days before the running nose and head cold, 14 days before the appearance of the rash.	8 to 14 days.	14 to 28 days.	10 to 25 days.	14 to 21 days.	1 to 7 days; varies with different germs.
EARLY SYMPTOMS	Starts with a running nose, bleary eyes and a hard cough. The doctor will look inside the mouth for minute white spots which appear 2 or 3 days before the rash.	Starts with "chestiness" and a simple cough. This later becomes spasmodic with "paroxysms" ending with a whoop and/or vomiting.	Generally off colour for a few days before they complain of pain or soreness on chewing.	First sign of the illness is usually the detection of spots on the trunk when the child is being bathed or undressed.	Some throat discomfort and slight fever at onset but the appearance of the rash is often the first sign of the disease. Painful swollen glands at the back of the head.	Nausea and vomiting often followed by diarrhoea. There may be fever.
DISTINCTIVE FEATURES	The rash appears 3 or 4 days after the first symptoms and begins behind the ears, spreads to the face and then downwards to the body and lower limbs. It consists of dark, purplish, spots which run together to make blotchy areas. The eyes are always reddened.	When fully developed diagnosis is obvious. Hurried breathing denotes onset of pneumonia. This may occur early in young children who have not been immunised and may leave permanent lung damage. Children with severe or frequent vomiting need more food after a paroxysm..	The salivary gland below the ear and be-hind the angle of the jaw is swollen and painful on pressure. The gland on the opposite side may be involved up to 7 days later. Boys after puberty may develop painful swelling of the testicles. Mild, transient meningitis is quite common, but it does not usually need special treatment.	The spots become "blistery" then yellow and form scabs. There may be several "crops" of spots.	The rash consists of pink flat spots which merge together to give a "peach-bloom" appearance. There is no red throat or pallor round the mouth.	Vomiting rarely lasts more than a day or two, but diarrhoea may persist. Crampy stomach pains are common, but very severe stomach ache, or blood in more than 2 or 3 motions need checking on by the doctor.
DURATION	Allow for a few days in bed and 2 weeks before they can return to school.	A severe attack will require at least 6 weeks before return to school but mild cases sometimes occur in children who have been immunised.	Only severe cases need to be confined to bed. Return to school after the swelling has subsided.	A child is no longer infectious as soon as ALL the spots have dried to scabs.	Uneventful recovery within 6 days. All German Measles patients should be isolated from pregnant women.	Usually 1 to 4 days. Severe cases may last many days. Solid foods need not be given until diarrhoea improves.
NURSING POINTS	The mouth needs special care with mouthwashes or swabbing after food. Shortness of breath as rash fades, persistent severe ear ache and very inflamed eyes usually require medical advice.	The small infant requires special care during paroxysms and should be lifted out of the cot and held head downwards until the spasm ceases. Older children should be calmed and reassured but can cope with their own spasms.	Careful washing of the mouth after a meal is important to remove all crumbs.	It is almost impossible to prevent the child from scratching the irritable spots so fingernails should be kept short.	The course of the disease is usually uneventful. Some patients develop pain and swelling in the small joints of the hands. This will subside.	Babies do best on frequent small breast feeds and plenty of boiled water. Otherwise make up electrolyte powder or tablets (from the chemist) in boiled water. Watered-down fizzy drinks may also be accepted by older children.

SEPTEMBER PLANNER

1
2
3
4
5
6
7
8
9
10
11
12
13
14
15
16
17
18
19
20
21
22
23
24
25
26
27
28
29
30

OCTOBER PLANNER

1
2
3
4
5
6
7
8
9
10
11
12
13
14
15
16
17
18
19
20
21
22
23
24
25
26
27
28
29
30
31

MEDICAL RECORDS

Use this page to keep a note of family medical records, such as dates of vaccinations and boosters.

NOVEMBER PLANNER

1
2
3
4
5
6
7
8
9
10
11
12
13
14
15
16
17
18
19
20
21
22
23
24
25
26
27
28
29
30

DECEMBER PLANNER

1
2
3
4
5
6
7
8
9
10
11
12
13
14
15
16
17
18
19
20
21
22
23
24
25
26
27
28
29
30
31

Our Family History

Tracing Your Family History

1. Living relatives.

   First-hand information is always the best. Your elderly relatives should be able to give you much information about their own families, their parents and grandparents, where they lived, what jobs they did and so on. Make a list of as many names as possible. They may have hoarded old documents, certificates and family photographs which will help you in your investigation.

2. OFFICIAL RECORDS

   General Register Office: The General Register Office, located in St Catherine's House, Kingsway, London WC2B 6JP, holds records dating back to 1st July 1837 for England and Wales. There is no charge for searching the indexes.

   You can request a copy of your own birth certificate, and from this you can work backwards, looking for both your parents' birth and marriage certificates, the marriage certificates of both sets of grandparents and so on. Once the entry has been found a full certificate can be supplied for a small fee.

   Scottish Record Office: If you were born in Scotland you will need to consult the Scottish Record Office (PO Box 36, HM General Register House, Edinburgh EH1 3YY).

   Local Parish Registers: For records of births, marriages and deaths before 1837 you will need to consult local parish registers which were first ordered to be kept in 1538. Not all parish registers have survived and many did not begin until the late 1600's. Most registers existing are in the hands of the clergy or locked for safe-keeping in the County or Diocesan Record Offices. Consulting these can be a lengthy process, especially in the larger cities, or if your family moved around the country a lot. However, there are some short-cuts. Phillimore and Co Ltd (Shopwyke Hall, Chichester, West Sussex PO20 6BQ) have published hundreds of parish registers thus minimizing the necessity for travelling all over the country. The Society of Genealogists (37 Harrington Gardens, London SW7 4JX) also holds many copies.

   To trace your ancestors you will thus need to know which parish they were born in. You can search for this in the census returns.

3. Census

   A census has been taken every 10 years from 1801 and returns for 1841, 1851 and 1861 are housed in the Public Records Office (Land Registry Building, Portugal Street, London WC2A 1LR) and can be inspected by the general public. The census return gives information as to where each person was born, indicating which parish registers should be targeted for your searches.

4. Other Denominations

   Parish registers did not cover Dissentors, Foreigners and Jews. Sources for these groups can be found in the 12 volume National Index of Parish Registers published by Phillimore & Co. The Index includes records for the following groups: Nonconformists, Presbyterians, Independents, Baptists, Society of Friends, Moravians, Methodists, Foreign Churches, Roman Catholics and for Jewish Genealogy.

   We wish you every success in your endeavour to trace your ancestors.

The Marriage

and

were joined together in marriage on

at

Our Genealogy

Husband's Full Name ....

Birth Date ....

Birth Place ....

Father's Full Name ....

Mother's Full Name ....

Brothers & Sisters ....

Wife's Full Name ....

Birth Date ....

Birth Place ....

Father's Full Name ....

Mother's Full Name ....

Brothers & Sisters ....

Our Children

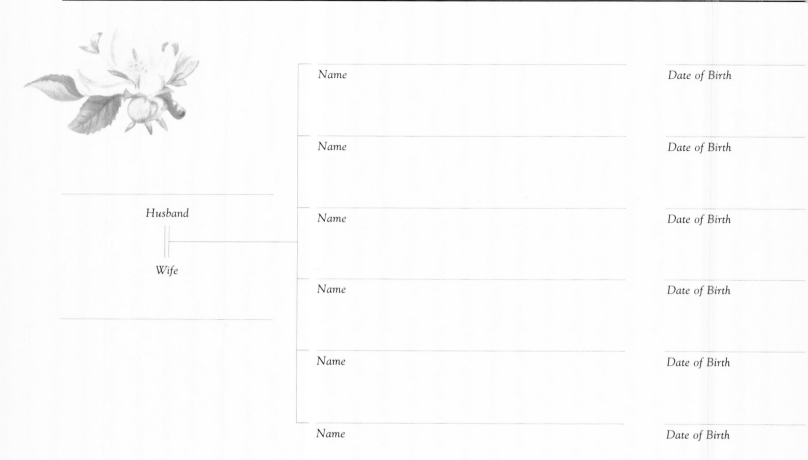

Husband

Wife

Name   Date of Birth

Name   Date of Birth

Name   Date of Birth

Name   Date of Birth

Name   Date of Birth

Name   Date of Birth

Spouse

Spouse

Spouse

Spouse

Spouse

Spouse

Our Grandchildren

Name	d.o.b.
Name	d.o.b.
Name	d.o.b.
Name	d.o.b.
Name	d.o.b.
Name	d.o.b.
Name	d.o.b.
Name	d.o.b.
Name	d.o.b.
Name	d.o.b.
Name	d.o.b.
Name	d.o.b.
Name	d.o.b.
Name	d.o.b.
Name	d.o.b.
Name	d.o.b.
Name	d.o.b.
Name	d.o.b.
Name	d.o.b.
Name	d.o.b.
Name	d.o.b.
Name	d.o.b.
Name	d.o.b.
Name	d.o.b.

Our Descendents

Include further details of your children, grandchildren and great grandchildren (the meaning of names chosen, birthdays, time and place of birth, and any other special details).

Husband's Ancestral Chart

Great Grandfather

Husband's Paternal Grandfather

Date & Place of Birth

Great Grandmother

Husband's Father

Date & Place of Birth

Great Grandfather

Husband's Paternal Grandmother

Date & Place of Birth

Great Grandmother

Great Great Grandfather

Great Great Grandmother

Great Great Grandfather

Great Great Grandmother

Great Great Grandfather

Great Great Grandmother

Great Great Grandfather

Great Great Grandmother

Great Great Great Grandparents

Great Great Great Grandparents

Great Great Great Grandparents

Great Great Great Grandparents

Great Great Great Grandparents

Great Great Great Grandparents

Great Great Great Grandparents

Great Great Great Grandparents

Husband's Ancestral Chart

Great Grandfather

Husband's Maternal Grandfather

Date & Place of Birth

Great Grandmother

Husband's Father

Date & Place of Birth

Great Grandfather

Husband's Maternal Grandmother

Date & Place of Birth

Great Grandmother

Great Great Grandfather

Great Great Grandmother

Great Great Grandfather

Great Great Grandmother

Great Great Grandfather

Great Great Grandmother

Great Great Grandfather

Great Great Grandmother

Great Great Great Grandparents

Great Great Great Grandparents

Great Great Great Grandparents

Great Great Great Grandparents

Great Great Great Grandparents

Great Great Great Grandparents

Great Great Great Grandparents

Great Great Great Grandparents

Wife's Ancestral Chart

Great Grandfather

Wife's Paternal Grandfather

Date & Place of Birth

Great Grandmother

Wife's Father

Date & Place of Birth

Great Grandfather

Wife's Paternal Grandmother

Date & Place of Birth

Great Grandmother

Great Great Grandfather

Great Great Grandmother

Great Great Grandfather

Great Great Grandmother

Great Great Grandfather

Great Great Grandmother

Great Great Grandfather

Great Great Grandmother

Great Great Great Grandparents

Great Great Great Grandparents

Great Great Great Grandparents

Great Great Great Grandparents

Great Great Great Grandparents

Great Great Great Grandparents

Great Great Great Grandparents

Great Great Great Grandparents

Wife's Ancestral Chart

Great Grandfather

Wife's Maternal Grandfather

Date & Place of Birth

Great Grandmother

Wife's Father

Date & Place of Birth

Great Grandfather

Wife's Maternal Grandmother

Date & Place of Birth

Great Grandmother

Great Great Grandfather

Great Great Grandmother

Great Great Grandfather

Great Great Grandmother

Great Great Grandfather

Great Great Grandmother

Great Great Grandfather

Great Great Grandmother

Great Great Great Grandparents

Great Great Great Grandparents

Great Great Great Grandparents

Great Great Great Grandparents

Great Great Great Grandparents

Great Great Great Grandparents

Great Great Great Grandparents

Great Great Great Grandparents

Husband's Family

Include details of brothers and sisters and their children.

Husband's Family

Include details of aunts and uncles and cousins (father's side).

Husband's Family

Include details of aunts and uncles and cousins (mother's side).

Husband's Family

Include details of great aunts and uncles and second cousins.

Wife's Family

Include details of brothers and sisters and their children.

Wife's Family

Include details of aunts and uncles and cousins (father's side).

Wife's Family

Include details of aunts and uncles and cousins (mother's side).

Wife's Family

Include details of great aunts and uncles and second cousins.

Special Occasions

Include weddings, christenings, important birthdays and family reunions.

Special Occasions

Special Occasions

Special Occasions

Special Occasions

Family Homes

Family Homes

Education and Special Achievements

Education and Special Achievements

Business Life

Business Life

Family Friends

Family Friends

Family Pets

Family Holidays

Family Holidays

Sporting Life

"Sports do not build character. They reveal it."

Heywood Broun

Clubs and Organisations

Hobbies and Interests

Special Memories

Use this section for any other notes about your family, for inserting special photographs and for keeping together newspaper clippings, certificates and so forth.

Special Memories

Important Family Dates

Keep a record of your own special family calendar, including birthdays, anniversaries, traditions etc.

Date   Event   Date   Event

....

....

....

....

....

....

....

....

....

....

....

....

....

....

....

....

Important Family Dates

Date   Event   Date   Event

....

....

....

....

....

....

CARD GAMES

CONTENTS

GAMES FOR TWO OR MORE PLAYERS

THINGS YOU NEED TO KNOW

THE PACK: a standard pack of cards has 52 cards, divided into 4 suits of 13 cards each. Each suit is clearly marked by its own symbol - Hearts, Clubs, Diamonds and Spades. Each card has a value. Ace is always either top or bottom, depending on the game. Then, from the top, the order is King, Queen, Jack, and the number cards from 10 to 1. There is an extra card, not used in all games, the Joker. Usually you can assign to him any value you want.

SHUFFLING AND CUTTING: at the start of every game, unless the rules say otherwise, the pack is shuffled, so that the cards are thoroughly mixed; and then cut. To cut the pack after it has been shuffled, get another player to lift around half of the shuffled pack, and place that half underneath, so that the upper half of the pack becomes the lower half.

RULES: card games are international, but often there are differences between the American and British versions of a game with the same name. In some cases it's not even the same game. The rules of some games can vary even within the same country. The important thing is to make sure that everyone in the game is playing to the same set of rules.

CUTTING AND DRAWING FOR DEALER: cutting for dealer is letting each player in turn cut the pack to show a card. Drawing is when each player draws a card from the pack. Normally the player with the highest card wins, though in some games it is the lowest. If there is a tie, the players involved try again.

GAMBLING: many card games can be used for gambling. Betting can take many forms: it doesn't have to be money. Currency can be anything from plastic chips to actual cash - whatever you use, don't bet what you haven't got.

CHOOSING YOUR GAME

Some card games are very straightforward and others are quite complex. Also, different people pick up rules and techniques at varying speeds. As a very general guide, the games in this book have been given an Easier/Harder rating. A single * indicates Easier, and more **s mean Harder. However, all the games in the book are well within the scope of the average person, even if you have never played before.

TECHNICAL TERMS OF CARD PLAY

Ace High: Ace is top scoring card.

Ace Low: Ace is lowest scoring card.

Ante: Also known as the Stake. The amount each player pays into the Pool at the start of a gambling game.

Available Card: In Patience, a card that can be used in play.

Build Up: In Patience, laying cards in ascending order of value on top of a Foundation Card.

Build Down: Laying the cards in descending order of value.

Chips: Tokens used in gambling games.

Column: Cards laid on the table in an overlapping vertical line.

Court Cards: Kings, Queens and Jacks.

Deal: Passing out cards to players. Most deals are one card at a time to each player, but this can vary according to the game.

Deck: Another word for the Pack.

Discard: In some games, to play a card of no value in the game, when the player cannot follow suit or play a trump. In other games, to play a card to the waste pile.

Eldest Hand: The player on the dealer's left, who normally leads.

File: In Patience, a column in the Layout, with cards overlapping but with suits and pip values visible. Files are built up towards the player.

Flush: A Hand of cards all of the same suit.

Follow Suit: To play a card of the same suit as the first card played in a trick.

Foundation Card: In Patience, a card laid down on which other cards are built up or down. They are normally aces or kings.

Hand: The cards held by a player at any point during the game. In Patience, it can also be any cards which have not been dealt out (also called the Stock).

Honour Cards: Ace, King, Queen and Jack of the trump suit.

Layout: The arrangement of cards in Patience games. Also called the Tableau.

Kitty: See Pool.

Lead: Being first player to set down a card. Also the card played first (lead card).

Meld: A set of three or more of a kind: e.g. either all Kings, or all Hearts (but these must be in sequence of pip value with no gaps).

Number Card: Card of any value between 10 and 2.

Pack: The full set of 52 cards (or 53 with a Joker). Also known as a Deck.

Packet: Set of cards that is less than a full Pack.

Pair: Two cards of the same kind, e.g. two 2's.

Pass: To miss a turn.

Pip Value: The number on a Number Card (e.g. a 9 has nine pips).

Pool: Total amount of cash or gambling chips staked in a game, usually placed in the middle of the table. Also called the kitty, or the pot.

Plain card: Card not of the trump suit.

Play: To play a card is to take it from your hand and use it in the game.

Rank: The value of a card.

Re-deal: In Patience, using the cards from the Waste Pile to deal again, when the Stock is used up.

Renege: To fail to follow suit in a game where following suit is not obligatory. Often confused with Revoke. See Revoke.

Revoke: To play an incorrect card, normally by failing to follow suit when able to; in a game when following suit is obligatory if you can do so. Often confused with Renege.

Round: This is complete once each player has played his cards in any trick.

Row: In Patience, a line of cards placed side by side (suit and pip value must always be visible if cards overlap).

Rubber: A set of games, especially in whist.

Ruff: A trump card. To ruff is to play a trump to a non-trump lead.

School: A group of players playing for money, especially in Poker.

Sequence: The order in which the cards run, from high to low, or the other way round.

Singleton: A single card of any suit.

Stock: The cards remaining after dealing, sometimes also called the Hand.

Tableau: Another word for Layout.

Talon: Another word for Waste Pile.

Trick: The cards played by all the players in a Round, one from each.

Trumps: Cards of a chosen suit that outrank all cards in all other suits during the game. Trumping is playing a trump card.

Waste Pile: Cards turned up in the course of playing Patience that are not available for play according to the rules of the game. Also sometimes called the Talon.

Wild Card: A card which a player can use to represent any other card (within the rules of the game).

♣ PATIENCE

These one-player games are all forms of Patience, also called Solitaire. You need a good-sized table to lay the cards out, though it is possible to find special Patience packs in a smaller size (these can also be useful for other card games when travelling).

ACCORDION *

The Aim: To be left with all the cards in one pile.

The Method: Use the standard 52-card pack. Deal out all the cards, face-up, in a single row, not overlapping. You can then move cards as follows:

Move a card on to the card on its left, if it is the same suit, or the same pip value. Move a card on to the card third from the left, if it is the same suit or the same pip value. After making a move, look to see if additional moves are now possible. When cards are stacked, don't just move the topmost card, but the whole stack, according to the value or suit of the topmost card.

♣ ACES UP **

The Aim: To be left with only the four Aces.

The Method: Use the standard 52-card pack. Cards rank in descending order from Ace to 2. Deal four cards in a row, face-up. If two or more cards of the same suit are dealt, discard the low or lower ones, leaving a space. Deal a further four cards face-up on top of the first ones, including the space(s). Again discard the lower cards of a duplicated suit. An eliminated card may uncover another that can also be eliminated. Once six deals have been made, you can move the top card or cards of any pile into a space, before the next deal. The aim is to discard all cards except the four Aces, and you finish with a row of four Aces.

Note: If a discard is at the top of a pile, only the top card is discarded.

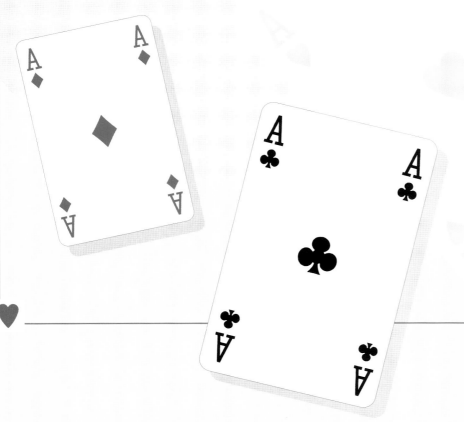

♣ BELEAGUERED CASTLE ✱✱✱

The Aim: To build up four piles in suit and sequence, Ace (low) to King.

The Method: Use the standard 52-card pack. Take out the four Aces and arrange them in a column (not overlapping). These are your foundation cards. The tableau is made by dealing six cards to each side of each of the Aces, alternately left and right, in overlapping rows. Only the outermost cards in each of these rows is available. These can be placed on the foundation pile if they form the next card in suit and sequence. Alternatively, they can be placed at the outer end of another row, but only in sequence of descending pip value; the suit does not matter. e.g. you can place a 5 of Hearts on a 6 of Spades. If a row is empty, any available card may be placed in it. In this way cards can be moved around, but this is still a tricky game to complete successfully.

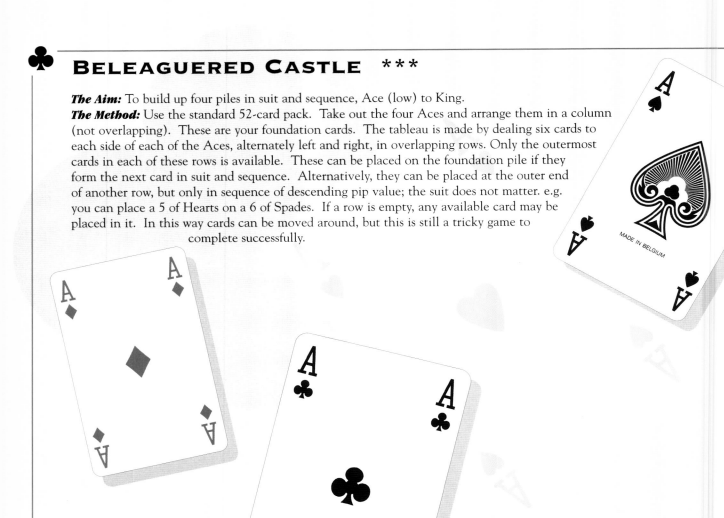

CANFIELD (ALSO KNOWN AS DEMON) **

This game is named after the American in whose casino it was invented.

The Aim: To complete the Foundations and Tableau.

The Method: Use the standard 52-card pack. Deal thirteen cards face-down in one pile, turn the pile face-up and place it at your left to form the stock. Deal the fourteenth card face-up and place it above and to the right of the stock pile. This is the first foundation card. Deal four more cards face-up in a row to the right of the stock, with the first card directly under the first foundation card. These form the tableau. The other three foundation cards are the other cards of the same pip-value as the first one. Place them next to the first, face-up, as they are turned up. The 34 cards remaining after the stock, first foundation card, and tableau cards have been dealt are placed face down, below the tableau. These form the Hand. The top three cards are turned over and laid alongside the hand. Only the top card of these three is available. If playable, it can be played on to a foundation pile or on to the tableau, and the card beneath becomes available. If not playable it forms the first card of the waste pile or talon. Once all possible cards are played, three more are turned over and placed on top of the talon.

When the Hand is exhausted, the talon is turned over, without being shuffled, and becomes the new Hand, cards taken in sets of three as before. This can be repeated indefinitely (sometimes it is restricted to three times only). Foundation piles are built up in suit sequence from the foundation card (e.g. 9, 10, J, Q, K, A, 2, 3, 4, 5, 6, 7, 8). Tableau piles are built up in the sequence of next-lowest rank and opposite colour (e.g. black 7 on top of red 8). A tableau pile must only be moved as a unit, on to a card of next highest rank and opposite colour to the bottom card of the unit. Spaces occurring in the tableau must be filled from the top card of the stock, or from the top of the talon if the stock is exhausted.

CASTLES IN SPAIN ***

The Aim: To build up suits, in sequence, from the foundation cards.

The Method: Use the standard 52-card pack. Deal a row of five cards, laying them face down from left to right. Above this row lay a row of four cards, then a row of three above that. Finally place one card above the centre card of the row of three. Then lay down two further sets, also face down, on top of the first set. You have thirteen cards left. Lay them face up, one by one, on top of the existing piles, keeping to the pattern. This makes thirteen depot piles. Any aces showing are played to the foundation row, once the tableau is set out. The card beneath the ace is turned up and becomes available for play. Available cards may be played either on to their foundation pile, or in descending sequence of alternate colour on another depot pile. Sequences or part sequences may be moved from one depot pile to another or to fill any spaces that are created. The cards may not be re-dealt.

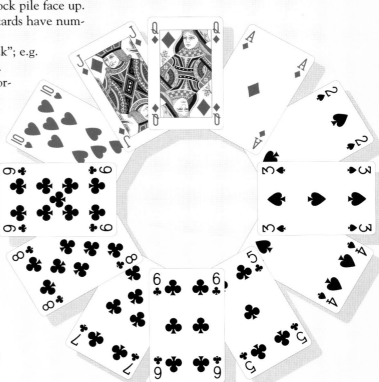

CLOCK PATIENCE *

The Aim: To arrange all the cards in clock-face formation, with the Kings in the centre.

The Method: Use the standard 52-card pack. Deal out thirteen packets of four cards, face-down. Place twelve of the packets in a circular formation, corresponding to the numbers on a clock face. Place the thirteenth packet in the centre of the "clock" to form the stock pile. Turn the top card of the stock pile face up.

If it is a Queen, it counts as 12; if a Jack, as 11; the other cards have numbers corresponding to their pip values.

The aim is to have them all at the right place on the "clock"; e.g. all four 6's at six o'clock; all four Queens at twelve o'clock. Aces go at one o'clock. Place the turned-up card in the correct position on the clock face, under the packet, face-up, and turn over the top card of that packet. Place that card in its right place in the same way, and turn over the top card of that packet, and so on. If you turn over a King, place him face-up at the bottom of the stock pile, and turn over the top card on the stock pile. Continue until four Kings have been turned up and placed in the stock pile. You win if the last card to be turned up is the fourth King, because by then you will have completed the clock.

♣ FLOWER GARDEN **

The Aim: To build up each suit in ascending sequence from its Ace (low Ace).

The Method: Use the standard 52-card pack and deal 36 cards, face-up, in 6 columns of 6, overlapping. These are your Garden. The bottom card of each column is available for play. Deal the remaining 16 cards in a face-up row. This is your Bouquet, and all cards in it are available at any time. As Aces become available, place them in a row above the Layout, face-up, and build up on them from 2 to King in each suit. You can create 4 auxiliary columns in which cards may be placed in descending order of suit, with available cards being played to the bottom of the column. When a column is used up, any available card can be used to start a new one.

Note: Only one card is moved at a time. When transferring cards from auxiliary column to foundation pile, cards may only be moved from the top of the auxiliary columns.

♣ GOLF **

The Aim: To completely clear the Tableau.

The Method: Use the standard 52-card pack. Deal a row of seven cards, face-up, then deal four more rows face-up on the first row; making a total of 35 cards, arranged so that all card values can be easily seen.

Turn up the first card from the Hand and lay it down face-up to form the Talon. Any card from the top layer of the tableau pile can be removed and placed on the talon, so long as it is in numerical sequence with the top card, whether upwards or downwards. Cards are turned up from the Hand, or stock, and placed on the talon. Cards in sequence may be played off the tableau on to the talon, so long as each pair of cards is in sequence, upwards or downwards. Suits do not matter. Laying down a King stops the sequence. Aces are low. Only a 2 may be placed on top of an Ace. The game is won if the Tableau can be completely cleared on to the Talon.

Scoring: Treat each deal as a golf hole. Each card remaining in your tableau at the end of a deal counts as a stroke. Par is a total of 36 in nine deals. If the tableau is cleared, any cards remaining in the stock count as one minus-stroke each, and are deducted from the running total.

KLONDIKE (ALSO KNOWN AS CANFIELD) **

The Aim: To build up on each Foundation card in suit and sequence, Ace (low) to King.

The Method: Use the standard 52-card pack. Deal one card face up and six others face down in a single row, left to right. Deal a card face-up on top of the second card, then five face-down on top of the others. Deal a card face-up on the third pile, and another four face down, and continue in this way until you have seven piles, the left-hand one consisting of just one card, face-up; the right-hand one consisting of one card face-up and six face-down.

Remaining cards are placed in a packet, face-down, to form the Stock. Aces (the Foundation Cards) should be placed in a row of four, separate from the seven piles, as they appear. Within the Layout, you build sequences of alternating colours - e.g. red, black, red - in descending order - e.g. a red 5 on a black 6, black 7 on red 8. King at the base of the pile. Cards can be transferred to their foundation piles, but cannot then be moved again. All face-up cards on a pile in the Layout must be moved as a unit. Whenever a card, or set of cards, is moved from one file to another, the face-down card that was beneath is turned over, and becomes available for play. When a space is made in the Layout, it can only be filled by a King. The top card of the Stock (kept face-down) is always available. Normally you would not try using it until you have made all possible moves with the cards in your Layout. You can move a stock card straight into a Foundation pile. If the card from Stock is not usable, it goes into the Waste Pile or Talon, face-up. When the Stock is used up, the talon can be turned over and used as stock. This is done once only.

SHAMROCKS **

The Aim: To build complete suit sequences from Ace to King on the Foundation Piles.

The Method: Use the standard 52-card pack. Deal all the cards into seventeen sets of three, spread out in fan-shapes so that suit and pip-value are clearly seen. There will be one single card left. This too goes face-up on the layout. If you have a king and another card of the same suit in one of your fans, put the King below the other. Uncovered cards are available for play. The first move must be to add a card to the single card. No fan is allowed to hold more than three cards. Aces as they appear should be moved beyond the layout, in a row of four, to form the bases of Foundation piles. When you have moved out all the cards from a fan, the space remains empty.

TOWER OF PISA   ***

The Aim: To end with a single file of cards descending in sequence from 10 to 2.

The Method: Use the standard 52-card pack, and remove a total of nine number cards, making a complete sequence from 10 to 2, in any mixture of suits. Lay them out in three columns of three. Discard the rest of the pack - it is not required. Once this is done, you can move cards. Only the bottom card of a column can be moved, and it can only be moved to the bottom of another column, and under a card of higher value. An empty file can be filled by the bottom card of either of the other two files.

Note: If you start with a 10 on the bottom row, try to use all the cards from one of the files, in order to have an empty file. Now you can move the 10 to the top (so long as it is still at the bottom of its file after your previous moves).

GAMES FOR TWO OR MORE PLAYERS

AUCTION PITCH **

This game is also known as Setback.

Number of Players: Two to eight, but four is best.

The Aim: To be first to gain seven points.

The Method: Use the standard 52-card pack. Aces are high. Cut for dealer (highest card). Dealer deals six cards to each player, from the left, in batches of three at at a time. Each player, beginning with eldest hand, bids for the number of points he expects to make in play. Each new bid must be higher than the previous one, except that the dealer, as last bidder need only match the previous bid, so long as it is less than four points. Players may pass rather than bid, and if all pass, the cards are gathered, shuffled and re-dealt by the same dealer. The highest bidder then declares trumps by "pitching" a card of that suit on to the table, face-up. Other players must follow suit if they can, or play a discard. Highest trump takes the trick, and the winner leads to the next trick. If a trump is again led, the same rule applies. If another suit is led, players may either follow suit or trump, but they can discard only if unable to follow suit. The highest card of the led suit wins, unless it is trumped. Play goes round until all tricks are taken.

Scoring: One point is given for each of:

High: The highest trump card played.

Low: The lowest trump card played.

Jack: The Jack of trumps.

Game: The highest value of scoring cards. The scoring cards are Ace (4); King (3); Queen (2); Jack (1) and 10 (10). Other cards have no scoring value. If the Jack is also highest or lowest trump played, it gets the extra points.

If a bidder fails to gain his bid, he is set back by the difference between his actual and his forecast score, which may end up in a minus figure, in which case he is "in the hole". The game is won by the first player to reach seven points, though by agreement this figure can be increased to a higher total. If two player make or exceed seven and one is the pitcher, the pitcher wins. If neither is the pitcher, the scores of each are counted in order to see who made seven first. No game point is given if two players tie for it.

Bidding "Smudge": A player who bids four, and makes it, is said to gain a smudge, or slam, and is awarded enough points to win the game outright (and any stakes that have been wagered). The only exception to this is if he was in the hole when making the bid, in which case he gains only the four points.

♣ AUTHORS *

Number of Players: From three to six, but four or five make the best number.

The Aim: To collect the most "books", i.e. sets of four cards all of the same rank.

The Method: Use the standard 52-card pack. Cut for dealer (highest card). The dealer deals out the full pack among the players; some may end up with a card less, but this does not matter. Play starts with the player to the left of the dealer. Looking at his hand, he decides what card to ask for. It must be of a rank in which he already has at least one card, from a different suit. He then chooses an opponent and addresses him by name, e. g. "George, please give me the 7 of Clubs". If George has that card, he must hand it over, and the asker's turn goes on until he asks for a card which an opponent does not have. The turn then passes to his left. When a player has all four cards of the same rank, he lays them face-down on the table, as a book. The winner is the one with most books. If playing for stakes, the winner of each book collects a chip from the other players. If a player asks for a card he already holds, or does not pass over a requested card when he has it, he pays a chip to each of the other players.

BEGGAR YOUR NEIGHBOUR *

Number of Players: Two.

The Aim: To win all 52 cards.

The Method: Use the standard pack of 52 cards. Cut for dealer (higher card). The non-dealer shuffles the cards. Each receives 26 cards. The cards should be set out in a pile, face down. Each player turns over the top card and places it in front of his pile. The higher card wins the other (Aces are low), and the player takes both cards and puts them face down. If two cards of the same value are turned over, then a 'war' is declared. The two equal cards are placed in the centre of the table. Each player makes a pile of three cards placed face-down, with a fourth on top, face-up. The higher of the face-up cards wins both piles, plus the two cards in the centre. If the two face-up cards are of equal value, the war is repeated, and the winner takes all the cards played. The game goes on until one player has all the cards.

♣ BLACKJACK ***

This game is the US form of Pontoon (see page 48).

Number of Players: Three to twelve, but four to six is best.

The Aim: To hit a total of 21, or as close as possible beneath it.

Card values: Ace: 1 or 11; King, Queen, Jack all 10; other cards by pip value.

The Method: Use the standard 52-card pack. Aces can be high or low. Cut or draw for dealer (lowest card). Dealer then deals a single card to each player, including himself. Having seen his card, each player places a bet on it (antes), up to an agreed maximum. The banker does not bet, but may double: if he does, any player unwilling to go double loses his stake. Players may also redouble. The banker then deals a second card all round. Any player then holding an Ace (11) or a court card or a 10 (10) has a "Natural 21" and the banker pays him double his stake, unless the banker also has a natural. In that case, the banker collects the player's stake, plus double the stake of any player who does not hold a natural. If no player has a natural, the banker then deals further cards from left, face-up, as the player calls for them.

The aim is to get to 21, or as near as possible, without going over (bust). The player can call "Stand" when he wants to stop, or say "Twist", or "Hit Me" if he wants to continue receiving cards. If the player is bust, the banker gets his stake. Players who have chosen to stand wait until the banker has dealt further cards to himself. If the banker goes bust, he pays the stake back to each standing player. If the dealer too stands, then each player shows his full Hand. The dealer pays off players with a total higher than his own (but less than 22) and collects from any with a lesser or the same total as himself.

Splitting: Players can split pairs, if his first two cards are of the same number value and rank (i.e. two Kings may be split, but not a King and a 10); he turns up the first card and treats each card as a separate Hand, on which he can draw, or stand. He must bet equally on each split Hand.

Doubling Down: If a player's first two cards come to a total of 11, he can turn his first card up, and call for another card to replace it, also doubling his bet. He must then stand on these three cards. The deal normally stays with the original banker, but he can sell the bank to the highest bidder before or after any Hand. But if a player has a natural, and the banker does not, then the player with the natural takes over the bank in the next hand. If more than one player has a natural, the one nearest the banker's left takes precedence.

BLACK MARIA **✴✴**

Number of Players: From three to six.

The Aim: To win tricks without winning any cards from the Hearts suit, or the Queen of Spades (Black Maria).

The Method: Use the standard pack of 52, but with three players, take out the 2 of Clubs. Always make sure that equal numbers of cards are dealt. Aces are high. Cut for dealer (lowest card). Dealing goes to the left. All cards are dealt out, one at a time. Once a player has seen his hand, he can place any three cards face-down, to be picked up by the player on his left; and he must pick up three from the player on his right. The opening lead is made by the player on the dealer's left. Other players must follow suit if they can; otherwise any card may be played. There are no trumps. The highest card of the leading suit wins. The winning player leads to the next trick. After each hand, the deal moves to the next player on the left.

Scoring: The aim is to avoid collecting hearts and to lose any Hearts that one is dealt. Each time a player takes a heart, he loses a point. At the end of the round, each player adds his score of Hearts, adding one for each Heart card he has. The lowest score wins the round. The game continues until one player reaches a score of fifty. The player with the lowest score is the winner.

Penalty Card: The Queen of Spades is treated as an additional Heart, but counting for 20 points.

Bonus card: The Jack of Diamonds can be treated as a bonus card, allowing a deduction of 10 points.

BRAG **

The most common form of Brag is Three-Card Brag.

Number of Players: Three to six.

The Aim: To win the pool by ending with the strongest Hand.

The Method: Use the standard 52-card pack. Aces are high, except for Ace, 2 3; when they are low. Stake limits are agreed at the start and cards are cut to find the dealer (highest card, with Ace high). Dealer antes his agreed stake, and deals three cards, one at a time, face-down, to each player. The remainder go face-up to his left.

Eldest Hand is first to bet, and may do so without looking at his cards. If he looks, he can then bet (holding his Hand) or drop out, in which case he places his cards on top of the stock. If he bets blind, he does not touch his cards. The turn passes to the left, and the player has the same choices, though if he bets it must be an amount equal to or greater than the previous bet, unless he is betting "open" and the previous bet was blind. In that case, he must bet at least double the previous one. If he bets blind and the one before him was open, he need only bet half. In a later round, a player may switch from betting blind to betting open. If he then decides to drop out, his cards go on the stock and his stake is lost. A player betting the same amount as the previous bet says "Stay" and names the sum. A player increasing the bet says "Raise" and names the sum. Play continues until only two players remain in play. If both are playing open, either may call to see the other's Hand, so long as he is at least matching the other's previous stake. On seeing the other Hand, the caller may then drop out, without showing his own Hand, and lose; or show that he has a better hand, and win. If one player is betting blind and the other is betting open, then the player betting open must continue to double the blind player's stake, or drop out. If both are betting blind, play continues until one does look at his cards. However it is possible for one blind player to call another; but not for an open player to call a blind one. The winner takes the pool.

Scoring:

Prial: Three of the same rank, e.g. 2-2-2.

Flush Run: Three in suit and sequence, e.g. 2-3-4 of Hearts.

Run: Any three in sequence, e.g. 2-3-4 of mixed suits.

Flush: Any three in the same suit.

Pair: Two of same rank plus a singleton, e.g. 2-2-9

High Card: No combination, but highest card, or second or third if there is a tie, wins.

In Pairs, a higher pair beats a lower pair, and equal pairs are decided by the singleton. Some players take a prial of 3-3-3 as beating any other; and also Ace-2-3 as beating Queen-King-Ace.

AMERICAN BRAG

In this form all Jacks and all 9's are Bragger's. These are all equal in value, and the highest Hand is a Hand of three bragger's. A combination including a bragger outranks a natural Hand of the same value. American Brag is more likely to result in a tie, in which case the pool is divided evenly.

BRIDGE ***

Also called Contract Bridge

Number of Players: Four, playing as two partnerships.

The Aim: To be the first side to win two games.

Method: Use the standard 52-card pack. Aces are high. It is usual to have a second pack, ready-shuffled, for the next dealer. Players sit with partners facing each other: North-South; East-West. Cut or draw for dealer. Before each deal, the pack is cut by the player to the dealer's right. The dealer then deals 13 cards to each player.

Bidding: Also known as the Auction, this starts with the dealer, who bids for the number of tricks he expects to take, along with his partner. He also specifies the trump suit, or states, "No trump". E.g. "Four Spades" means he expects to score four tricks with Spades as trumps. Scoring only begins after six tricks have been won, and the lowest bid is One (i.e. one more than six). Bids run in ascending order: Clubs, Diamonds (the minor suits) Hearts, Spades (major suits), and No Trumps. Lowest bid is one Club; highest is seven No Trumps. Alternatively, a bidder can Pass (no tricks over six). Bidding moves to the left. If all pass, Hands are turned in and the deal moves to the left. If a bid is made, the next player can raise it (e.g. from one Spade to two Spades) or go higher (e.g. one Heart over one Diamond). A player may double a bid made by the opposing team: this means that if they make the bid, they score double trick points; if they fail, the opposing side gets the trick points. The next player to call can over call (make a higher bid) or redouble the already-doubled bid, which redoubles the potential gain for either side. Players do not double or redouble their own partner's bids. Players may re-bid, but when three have "passed" in a row, bidding stops.

At the end of bidding, the last to bid becomes the Declarer, and plays the Hand for the bidding team, unless he names the same trump suit (or no trumps) as his partner did, in which case the partner becomes Declarer. The declaring side must win at least as many tricks as they bid; the defending side tries to prevent them.

Play begins with the opponent on the declarer's left, who leads with any card. The declarer's partner then lays his hand face-up on the table, arranging it in suits, in descending order from the Aces. This enables the declarer to play it as a "dummy" Hand whilst also playing his own Hand: his partner cannot assist. Play goes to the left; players must follow suit if they can; otherwise they may either trump or play a discard. Highest card of the suit led, or highest trump, takes the trick. The winner of the trick leads to the next, and so on until all thirteen tricks are taken.

Scoring: tricks are scored in ascending value, according to the trump suit, or No Trumps. In Clubs and Diamonds, each trick scored (from the 7th) counts as 20 points. In Hearts and Spades, each trick scored counts as 30 points. With No Trumps, the first trick scored is at 40 points, with 30 points for each additional bid. If the bid has been doubled, the scores are doubled, and multiplied by 4 if redoubled. The first side to score 100 trick points wins, and play resumes in a fresh game. The rubber ends if the same team wins two games in a row; otherwise it is best of three.

Scoring Method: Both sides keep the score for the other side as well as for themselves, to ensure accuracy. A special sheet is used, or can be drawn up, with a column for each side (WE and THEY) and a horizontal line across the middle. Trick points (including doubles) are entered below this line, and bonus points above it. Bonus points are awarded for tricks won over and above the contract; for winning a contract to take 12 tricks (Small Slam) or 13 tricks (Grand Slam); and for defeating a contract. Bonus points are also awarded to players who happen to get the honour cards (Ace down to 10) of the trump suit, or all four Aces if the call is No Trumps. This applies to the player's own hand, not to the combined hands of the partnership.

The side to win the first game of a rubber is then called "vulnerable" and different scoring rates apply to it (see Scoring Table).

SCORING TABLE FOR CONTRACT BRIDGE

DECLARER'S SIDE, BELOW THE LINE SCORE

FOR EACH ODD TRICK OVER SIX	ORDINARY CONTRACT	DOUBLED	REDOUBLED
Minor Suits	20	40	80
Major Suits	30	60	120
No Trump: first trick	40	80	120
Further tricks	30	60	120

DECLARER'S SIDE, ABOVE THE LINE SCORE

	NOT VULNERABLE Minor Major & NT		VULNERABLE Minor Major & NT		MAKING CONTRACT
Each overtrick	20	30	20	30	No bonus
When doubled	100	100	200	200	50
When redoubled	200	200	400	400	50
Small Slam	500	500	750	750	
Grand Slam	1000	1000	1500	1500	

DEFENDER'S ABOVE THE LINE SCORE WHEN DECLARERS FAIL TO MAKE CONTRACT

	NOT VULNERABLE All Suits & NT	VULNERABLE All Suits & NT
Each undertrick	50	100
Doubled: 1st undertrick	100	200
Each further undertrick	200	400
Redoubled: 1st	200	400
Each further undertrick	400	600

WINNER'S BONUS POINTS (ABOVE THE LINE)

WIN RUBBER IN 2 GAMES	RUBBER IN 2 OUT OF 3 GAMES	ONE GAME, RUBBER UNFINISHED	PART SCORE, RUBBER UNFINISHED
700	500	300	50

BONUS POINTS FOR HONOUR CARDS HELD

TRUMP SUIT 4 IN ONE HAND	NO TRUMPS (ALL THE ACES) 5 IN ONE HAND	ALL IN ONE HAND
100	150	150

Conventions: Effective bridge play means that the players in the two partnerships must use the same "language": during the auction they cannot see each other's Hands and have to rely on applying the same bidding pattern to get an understanding of what each is holding. There are numerous systems, and entire books have been written about each one. Probably the most straightforward is to assign points to individual cards, once you have sorted your hand into its suits, in descending order of value from left to right. Count 4 for each Ace, three for each King, two for each Queen and one for each Jack. These are your high-card points. Normally a partnership will have a combined strength of around 20. With 25 in high cards you should win the game; with 37 you should achieve a Grand Slam. If your high cards come to less than 13, leave the opening bid to your partner.

Four or more cards of the same suit in your Hand make a long suit; 3 or less a short suit. Count an extra point for any fourth or more card in a side (non-trump) suit, and any fifth or more card in a trump suit. To open with a suit bid of one (naming trumps) you should hold 12 to 14 points in that suit. With two biddable suits, bid the longer; if they are of equal length, bid the higher-scoring one. For a trump bid of two, you need at least 7 cards in your trump suit and a value of 22. This is a very strong signal to your partner.

The most common opening bid is one trick, and the partner's responding bid must convey a message back about the strength of his own Hand, which will then determine what happens in the next round of bidding. He can raise in the same suit, make a higher bid in a new suit, or bid No Trumps. If he has at least three cards of the first bidder's named trump suit, he can safely raise the bid to two. Cautious bidding should be the rule until you have got a feeling for the game - and an understanding with your partner. It is a good idea to practice bidding patterns outside the framework of an actual game.

CATCH THE TEN, OR SCOTCH WHIST *

Number of Players: Two to eight.

The Aim: To win tricks, especially with the top five trumps.

The Method: Use a 36-card pack, with Ace high, and 2 to 5 omitted. Remove any 6 if five to seven are playing; include the 5 if eight are playing. Cut for dealer (highest card). Dealer deals out the full pack, one card at a time, giving a total of nine each if four are playing; seven each to five; six each to six; and five each to seven or eight. The dealer turns up the final card to show trumps, before taking in into his own Hand.

Eldest Hand leads, and other players, from the left, must follow suit if they can, otherwise trump or play a discard. The trick is won by the highest card of the suit led, or by the highest trump. The winner of a trick leads to the next.

Scoring: The top five cards in the trump suit are: Jack (11); Ace (4); King (3); Queen (2) and 10 (10). No other cards have value. When all tricks are taken, each player counts the value of the trumps in his set of tricks, and also adds one point for every card he now has in addition to the cards he was originally dealt.

♣ CHEAT! *

Number of Players: Three upwards.

The Aim: To be first to get rid of all the cards in your Hand.

The Method: Use the standard 52-card pack. Cut for dealer (highest card). The dealer deals all the cards among the players, one at a time. The player to the dealer's left leads, by placing face-down one or more cards. He says what the cards are - but he is not obliged to tell the truth about the number of cards, their suit or their value. An opposing player may call "Cheat!" at any point. The last player has then to turn his discards face-up. If it turns out that he was cheating, he has to pick up all the cards in the discard pile. If he was not, the caller must take all the discards. If there is no call, the next player to the left takes his turn, placing his cards face-down on top of the cards already played. He can play only cards of the same value as those just announced, or the next rank up (Ace if it was a King, 2 if it was an Ace). But - he may cheat. The game goes on in this way until one player has successfully laid down all his cards.

cheat !

CRAZY EIGHTS **

Number of Players: Can be played by two, but three to five is better, and seven or more is possible.

The Aim: To be first to get rid of all one's cards, and to reach 500 points.

The Method: Use the standard 52-pack; two packs shuffled together if seven or more are playing. Cut for dealer (highest card). Dealer deals five cards to each player, from his left, one at a time. The remaining cards form the stock, face-down, with the top card turned face-up and laid alongside to start the discard pile. Starting with the player on the dealer's left, each player either puts down a playable card face-up on the discard pile, or, if no card is available, draws an additional card from stock. Playable cards depend on what the top card on the discard pile is. If it is not an 8, any card may be played which matches the suit or is equal in rank. If it is an 8, then any card of the same suit may be played. An 8 may be played at any time, and the player who leads it can name any suit to go next. The first player to go out (i.e. put down all his cards) calls out "Crazy eights!" and wins the round. First player to reach 500 points wins the game.

Scoring: The winner of a round scores 100.
Penalty scores for players with cards in hand are as follows:

Eight: 50

Any Court card: 10

Other cards: Face value

Variants: To add a touch of complexity, a player who is down to one card must knock on the table to indicate this, or else pick up two cards from the stock. If the player before you puts down a Queen (or other previously decided card) you miss that turn. When an Ace is played, reverse the direction of play.

FAN-TAN **

Number of Players: Three to Eight.

The Aim: To get rid of all your cards.

The Method: Each player starts off with an equal number of chips, and puts a chip into the pool at the start. Use the standard pack of 52 cards. Choose the dealer by someone dealing cards face-up; the first to get a Jack becomes the dealer. The dealer shuffles, and player to his right cuts. Cards are dealt one at a time, from the dealer's left; until the pack is used up. Play begins from the dealer's left. The first card to be played must be a 7. If you have no seven you pass, and pay a chip to the pool. When a 7 is put down, the 6 and 8 of the same suit are also available for play, and once these are down, the next values above and below can be played. The four 7's are laid in a row in the centre of the table, with the 6's to one side and the 8's to the other. Suits can then be built up to the King and down to the Ace, which is low. Only one card can be played in each turn. If you can play a card, you must. If you pass when able to play, pay a penalty of three chips to the pool. The first player to lay down all his cards wins. Others pay one chip for each card they are left holding; and the winner then takes the whole pool.

FIVE HUNDRED ***

Number of Players: Two to six, but three is the ideal number.

The Aim: To make, or beat, the contract; and be first to score 500 points.

The Method: Use a pack of 32 cards (standard pack excluding all cards between 2 and 6, inclusive), plus a Joker. Draw for first deal: lowest card wins (Ace is low, Joker lowest). Deal to the left, ten cards to each player in packets of 3-4-3. After the first round of 3, three cards are laid face-down in the centre. This is the widow. Having seen their Hands, each player may make a single bid, or pass. Each bid states the number of tricks the player will take, from six to ten; and his trump suit (or No Trumps), e. g. "eight diamonds"; "ten no trump". Each bid must be for a higher number of tricks than the bid before, or the same number if ten. The highest bid, or first to bid ten, becomes the contract. If no-one makes a bid, the dealt cards are collected, shuffled and re-dealt by the next dealer (player to the dealer's left).

Bidding then resumes. The other two players combine in alliance to defeat the bidder, but they may not see each other's Hands. The bidder takes up the widow, then discards any three cards from his Hand. He can lead with any card. The others must follow suit, if able; if they can't, any card may be played. The trick is won by the highest trump, or highest card of the suit led. The winner of the trick leads to the next trick. If the bidder had called No Trumps, then the only trump is the Joker. The trick can only be won by the highest card of the suit led, unless the Joker is played, when it wins. If a player leads with the Joker, he must declare the suit that the others must follow, if they can.

Trumps: The ranking of suits, high to low, is: Hearts, Diamonds, Clubs, Spades. But a No Trump bid outranks them all.

Card ranking in the trump suit: Joker; Jack; Jack of the other suit of the same colour; ace; King; Queen; 10; 9; 8; 7.

Card ranking in the non-trump suits: Ace, King, Queen, Jack (but see above); 10; 9; 8; 7.

Scoring: Each player keeps a running total from round to round. The bidder's opponents keep their scores separately. See the table for the number of points awarded.

If the bidder makes his contract, he scores the value of his bid. If his bid adds up to less than 250, and he actually takes all ten tricks, he is awarded only 250. If he is set back (fails to make his contract), then the value of his bid is subtracted from his running total. This can produce a minus figure. Each opponent scores 10 points for every trick he wins.

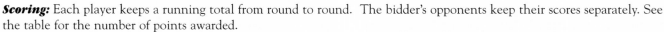

	NUMBER OF TRICKS BID				
	6	7	8	9	10
NO TRUMP	120	220	320	420	520
HEARTS	100	200	300	400	500
DIAMONDS	80	180	280	380	480
CLUBS	60	160	260	360	460
SPADES	40	140	240	340	440

Game is made at 500. If another player goes out (hits 500) in the same deal as the bidder, the bidder wins.

Variant: A player may bid "nullo". This is an offer to win no tricks, at No Trump. Its scoring value is 250, so its bid value is between eight clubs and eight spades. If the nullo bidder gains the contract, he loses if he wins a single trick. Each opponent gains 10 points for each trick made by the bidder.

FROGS IN THE POND *

Number of Players: Two.

The Aim: To be first to score 100 points, by winning tricks.

The Method: Use the standard 52-card pack. Cut for dealer (highest card). The dealer deals ten cards to each, two at a time. He then deals ten cards face down in the centre of the table: these are the "frogs in the pond".

The dealer then leads a single card. The opponent must follow suit, from his ten cards; if he cannot the penalty is 10 points, and the dealer takes the trick. Alternatively, if the opponent can follow suit, he wins 10 points.

The winner of each trick takes the cards played, plus one frog, which goes face down on the trick gained. The winner then leads for the next trick.

There are no trumps.

Players keep the tricks they have won. When all cards are played, the score - including frogs - is added up, and another round begins.

Scoring: The only cards with scoring value are Tens: 10; Fives: 5; Aces: 4; Kings: 3; Queens: 2; Jacks: 1. All others: nil.

Note: In the basic version you only have to follow suit to win the trick, even if you play a lower card. It is also possible to play so that the higher card in the led suit wins the trick.

GERMAN WHIST **

Number of Players: Two

The Aim: To build a winning Hand and score 50 points.

The Method: Use the standard 52-card pack. Cut for dealer (highest card).

Dealer then deals 13 cards alternately to each player. The 27th card is turned over to denote trumps for the game. The remaining cards form the stock, face down.

The dealer leads a card, and the opponent can either beat it with a higher card of the same suit, or any trump (if trumps were not played), or play a lower card and lose the trick. The winner of the first trick takes the face-up trump card, waits for his opponent to draw a fresh card from the stock, then turns over the next card. When all the stock has been played, the players' hands are played out, with the winner of the previous trick taking the lead.

Scoring: One point per trick. The winning score is normally 50, though this can be varied by agreement.

223

♣ GIN RUMMY **

Number of Players: Two.

The Aim: To build up a winning Hand of Melds and be first to score 100 points.

The Method: Use the standard 52-card pack (Ace is low). Cut for dealer.

Dealer shuffles, and deals ten cards to each player. The remaining cards are placed face-down to form the stock.

The top card is turned face-up, and placed by itself, to start the discard pile. The other player has the option of taking that card, or refusing it; he cannot draw a card from the stock pile. If he refuses it, the turn goes to the dealer. If the dealer also passes (refuses the turned-up card) the other player may take the top (face-down) card from stock.

When a card is picked up, another must be placed on the discard pile.

The aim is to be the first to lay down all your cards in melds (sets of three or more cards of the same suit in consecutive numbers, counting from Ace as low; or sets of three or more from different suits but the same value).

If you have a full hand of melds, call out "Gin!" or knock on the table. You receive a bonus of 25 points plus the value of your opponent's unmelded cards. You can also choose to go out if you have some melds and the unmelded cards in your hand have a value of 10 points or less. In this case, however, your opponent has the chance to "lay off" available cards on your melds, and complete his melds using your unmelded cards before the score is counted. The player with the lower value of unmelded cards receives a 25 point bonus. If neither player has gone out before the last two cards are drawn from the stock, the round is treated as a no-score draw.

Scoring: Court Cards (King, Queen, Jack): 10 points each. Ace: one point. Number cards: as their number value. The value of the unmatched or unmelded cards still in your hand counts against you. If the player who went out has the same, or greater value of remaining cards as his opponent, the opponent gets a ten-point bonus plus the difference between the card values. The winner of the game is the first to reach 100 points.

Go Boom *

Number of Players: Two to six.

The Aim: To be first to get rid of all one's cards.

The Method: Use the standard pack of 52 cards. Cut for dealer (highest card). The dealer deals seven cards, one at a time, to each player. The rest of the pack is placed face-down and forms the stock.

Eldest Hand (the player to the dealer's left) leads. Other players must follow suit, or play a card of the same face value as the lead (Aces are high). A player who has no playable card must draw from the stock until he receives a playable card. Once the stock is used up, players with no playable card must pass (wait for the next trick to be played). The trick is won by the highest card of the suit led. The winner of a trick leads to the next trick. Tricks are piled into a discard pile since they have no scoring value. The first player to have no cards left is the one who "Goes Boom" and wins the game.

HONEST JOHN *

Number of Players: From two to twelve.

The Aim: To bet on the chance of turning up a higher card than the banker's.

The Method: Use the standard pack of 52 cards. Aces are high. Cut for dealer, who is also banker (highest card).
Dealer cuts the pack into from four to six separate piles, face-down. Each player places a chip against his chosen pile, leaving one pile vacant for the banker. The banker turns over the top card of his pile. From the banker's left, the players now turn over the top cards of their piles, in turn. For any card that is of lower value than the banker's, or matches it, they pay their chip to the banker. The banker pays a chip for any card of higher value than his own.   All suits are equal. The bank moves to the left after each hand is completed.

KNAVES *

Number of Players: Three.

The Aim: To win the greatest number of tricks, without taking any Jacks.

The Method: Use the standard 52-card pack. Aces are high. Cut for dealer (highest card). The dealer deals seventeen cards to each player, one card at a time. The left-over card is turned over to denote trumps for the round. The player to the dealer's left leads by laying down a card. Other players must follow suit, trump, or discard a card.

Scoring: Each trick won receives one point. The first player to reach twenty points wins the game.
But any trick containing a Jack is penalised by deducting points as follows: Jack of Hearts four; Diamonds three; Clubs two; Spades one.

KNOCK-OUT WHIST *

Number of Players: From three upwards.

Aim of the Game: To win the greatest number of tricks.

How to Play: Use the 52-card pack. Aces are high. Cut for dealer (highest card). The dealer then deals seven cards to each player. The rest of the cards are placed face-down, but the top one is turned over to determine trumps. Aces are high. The player to the dealer's left leads the first card. Players must follow suit if they can, otherwise they may play any card. In the second round six cards are dealt (and five in the third round, down to one in the final round).

The winner of a round calls trumps for the next, after the deal. In the seventh round, when only one card is dealt to each player, the players cut for trumps.

A player who takes no tricks in any round is "knocked" out and takes no more part in the game. However, the first player to take no tricks is awarded the "dog's chance". He is dealt one card in the next round, and can play it to the trick of his choice. If he does not play it to a particular trick, he knocks on the table, and play passes to the next in turn. If he wins a trick, he is fully back in the game for the next round. The game can be won in any round after the third if one player takes all the tricks.

LOO *

Number of Players: From three to nine.

The Aim: To win tricks.

The Method 1: Single Pool. Use the standard pack of 52 cards. Aces are high.

Players put an agreed number of chips or coins into the pool. These must always be equally divisible by three.

Any player distributes cards until a Jack is dealt: the recipient of the Jack is first dealer.

Trumps are not determined immediately. If all players are able to follow suit in each of the three leads, trumps are not called. But as soon as someone fails to follow suit, once that trick is completed, then the top card of the stock pile is turned face-up to determine trumps for each subsequent trick. Three cards are dealt, one at a time, to each player, starting to the dealer's left. The player to the dealer's left leads. Others must follow suit if they can, otherwise they may trump (see above). Tricks are not gathered together: the cards are left face-up in front of the players.

Scoring: Each winning trick is entitled to win one third of the pool in each round. Players with no tricks are looed. They must put a double stake into the pool for the next round.

Method 2: Double Pool. In this method, an extra hand, known as the Miss, is dealt, to the right of the dealer. The top card of the stock is turned up to determine trumps. Before the opening lead, each player must tell the dealer whether he will stand, pass, or take the Miss. To stand is to remain in play, and participate in the tricks. To pass is to go out of play: the player's cards are placed face-down under the stock. To take the Miss is to pick up the extra hand and to place your original hand face-down under the stock. If you take the Miss you cannot then pass, and must remain in play. If all players pass except the dealer, or a player who has taken the Miss, the lone player takes the whole pool.

If only one player ahead of the dealer stands, then the dealer must either stand, or take the Miss, and "defend" the pool. In Double Pool the leader to each trick must play a trump if he has one; and if he has the Ace of trumps, that must be led first. If the Ace was turned up and he has the King, then that must be led first.

Scoring: As before, with each trick taking one third of the pool. Where the dealer has had to "defend" the pool, he neither collects nor pays, but his opponent, depending on his score, does one or the other.

NAP, OR NAPOLEON **

Number of Players: From two to six, but four or five make the best game.

The Aim: As highest bidder, to win the contracted number of tricks.

The Method: Use the standard pack of 52 cards. Aces are high, except when drawing for the deal, when they are low. Lowest card is first to deal and has choice of seat, with second-lowest on his left, and so on. Players pay an agreed number of tokens or coins into the pool. The dealer deals out five cards, one at a time, to each player, starting on his left. On receipt of the cards, each player, starting on the dealer's left, must make a bid for the number of tricks that he will win, if he gets the chance to name the trump suit. Each must either bid higher than the previous bid, or pass.

If all pass, the dealer must make the minimal bid of at least one trick. Otherwise, the lowest acceptable bid is two.

To bid for all five tricks is to go Nap. The highest bidder makes the opening lead, and the suit he leads automatically becomes trumps. Others must follow suit if they can, or play a discard. The highest trump, or if No Trump is played in following suits, the highest card of the leading suit wins. The winner leads to the next trick. The other players set out to play against the highest bidder. If the highest bidder wins tricks over and above his bid, he receives no credit.

As soon as he has won his forecast number of tricks, he must show his remaining cards to prove that he has not revoked at any point.

Scoring: If Nap is made, it is worth ten points to the winner. If, having bid Nap, the player fails to make it, he pays five points to the other players. If the player makes his bid, but it is less than Nap, it is worth as many points as there are tricks; if he is defeated, he pays the same number of points, to each of his opponents.

Deals are settled at the end of each round.

Note: 1. Bidding can be increased if players are allowed to bid a Wellington. This is a bid to go Nap, but also doubling all the stakes. A player can only do this if Nap has already been bid.

2. Bidding misere. This is a bid to take no tricks, which can be made by a player with no trumps.

It exceeds a bid for three tricks but is itself exceeded by a bid for four. It offers a player with a poor hand an opportunity to stay in the game.

OH HELL **

Number of Players: From three to seven can play, but four are best.

The Aim: To achieve exactly the number of tricks you predict or "bid".

The Method: Use the standard 52-card pack. Each player plays for himself alone; there are no partners. Cut for dealer (highest card); dealer also chooses where to sit. Others sit from the dealer's left in descending order of card drawn. The first deal is one card each. Each subsequent deal is increased by one card each until the thirteenth and last, when the full pack is dealt out (always in equal hands: leftover cards in the last deal are not used). After each deal, except the last one, the next card is turned up to determine trumps. In the final deal there are no trumps. Each player, starting from dealer's left, must make a bid, predicting the number of tricks he will take. This can include Zero, or Pass. Bids, also known as Contracts, are recorded on paper by a score keeper, who at the end of bidding announces whether the total number of bids is Over, Under or Even with the number of winnable tricks in the round. The player to the dealer's left leads. Other players must follow suit, or if unable to do so, may play any card including a trump. The winner of a trick leads to the next trick.

Scoring: A player who achieves his exact Contract scores ten, plus the amount of his bid. A player who achieves either more or less than his bid "busts" and receives no points.

OLD MAID *

Number of Players: Two to five.

The Aim: To avoid being left holding the last remaining Queen.

The Method: Cut for dealer (highest card). Set aside the Queen of Clubs from a 52-card deck, and deal out the remaining 51 cards (no matter if one player has an extra card). Each player's cards are spread out, face-up, and any pairs are removed and placed face-up in the centre of the table. Each player then shuffles his remaining cards and holds them facing away from the others. Players take it in turn, left to right, to lay their cards on the table, face-down, for the player to the left to select one. If it enables him to make a pair, he discards the pair; if not, he keeps it.

Then it is his turn to offer his cards to the player on his left. Eventually all the cards will be paired except for the one remaining Queen - The Old Maid - and whoever is left with it loses the round. Play continues for an agreed number of rounds, with the winner being the one to win the most rounds.

♣ PIP-PIP *

Number of Players: Three to seven.

The Aim: To score points for changing the trump suit, and for capturing certain cards.

The Method: Use two standard 52-card packs, thoroughly shuffled together. Cut for dealer (highest card), and cut again to identify trumps. Dealer deals seven cards to each player and places the remainder face-down as the stock. Eldest hand leads to the first trick and others must follow suit if they can, or trump, or discard from another suit. The trick is taken by the highest card of the suit led, or by the highest trump (see Scoring values). If two identical cards are played, the second beats the first.

The winner of a trick draws the top card from the stock and adds it to his hand, and other players, from his left, do the same. When there are not enough cards left in the stock to go round, no more cards are drawn, and hands are played until all cards are gone.

Changing trumps: Just before a card is led to a new trick, a player with a King and Queen of the same suit (so long as it is not the trump suit) in his hand can turn that suit into trumps by saying "Pip-pip", and laying the cards face-down on the table. They continue to be playable as part of his hand. This earns a bonus of 50 points.

If two players call "Pip-pip" before the same trick, both get 50 points, but the later call becomes trumps. A player can call "Pip-pip" twice for the same suit, so long as he has both Kings and both Queens.

Scoring: The only cards with scoring values are:

2's (deuces): 11; Aces: 10; Kings: 5; Queens: 4; Jacks: 3. Others: nil.

Each player adds up his card-score and his piping score at the end of each round, and the highest score is the winner.

POKER ***

There are two basic forms of Poker; Draw and Stud Poker, and each has many variants. However, there are certain standard features, and once you know these, it are easy to learn any adaptation of the game.

Number of Players: 3 or more. Five to eight is best for Draw Poker, seven to ten for Stud Poker.

The Aim: To have the highest-ranking hand at the end of the game.

The Method: Use the standard 52-card pack. Aces can be high or low. The suits are all of equal value.

Scoring: All poker hands consist of five cards. Depending on your hand, you score it as follows (highest to lowest):

Straight Flush: Five cards in suit and sequence, with Ace being either high or low. **A**

Royal Flush: (Ace-high, King, Queen, Jack, 10 straight flush) beats any other.

Four of a Kind: Four cards of the same value (e.g. four Queens or four 4's), plus any other card. A higher-ranking set beats a lower-ranking one.

Full House: Three of one kind and a pair of another kind (e.g. three Queens and two 4's). A higher-ranking set beats a lower-ranking one.

Flush: Five cards all of the same suit but not making up a complete sequence. If two players have flushes, the one with the higher top card wins. If the top cards match,then highest second card wins, and so on.

Straight: Five cards in complete sequence of rank, with Ace either high or low, but of different suits. Higher top card beats a lower one.

Three of a Kind: Three cards of the same value, plus two others which are not a pair. A higher-ranking set beats a lower-ranking one.

Two Pairs: Two sets of two of the same value, plus any other card. Highest ranks win if two players have Two Pairs.

One Pair: Two cards of the same value, the others all singletons. Highest ranked pair or highest singleton wins.

High Card: Any hand which is not one of those listed above. Highest value wins.

If nobody has a Pair or better, then the highest card wins.   If there is a tie for highest, then the next highest wins, and so on.

Introducing Wild Cards, either by having a Joker, or naming the deuce (2) as wild, extends the range of possibilities. Five of a Kind now becomes top scorer, with four Aces plus the wild card beating any other combination.

♣ DRAW POKER

To choose the dealer, any player distributes cards from a shuffled pack: first to get a Jack becomes the first dealer. The cards are shuffled three times, lastly by the dealer, and the player to dealer's right cuts.

Cards are dealt one at a time, from the dealer's left, until each player has five cards.

Betting: Stakes should be agreed in advance (cash or chips). Each player places a chip in the pool at the start.

One player acts as Banker. Betting normally starts to the dealer's left and goes clockwise. In some schools, no player is allowed to open the betting unless he holds a pair of Jacks or a higher combination. You can either call, raise or fold (sometimes called drop). If you fold, you discard your hand and lose your stake. If you call, you must put into the pool enough chips to match, but not exceed, what any other player has bet in that round. If you raise, you add more value to the call amount, subject to an agreed upper limit. When you raise, you must say clearly the amount you are raising by. Once everyone has made a bet, or folded, the players still in the game may discard up to three cards, and receive replacement cards from the dealer. Another betting round follows and the players again call, raise or fold.

Previous bets cannot be withdrawn. At the end of each betting round, each player has to have put the same amount into the pool. Players who don't do this, must fold.

The Showdown: This is when hands are shown. The highest hand (see Scoring) wins the pot.

STUD POKER

Arrangements for ante-ing stakes and choosing dealer as for Draw Poker.

Five-Card Stud: The dealer deals a round of cards face-down (the "hole-card"), then a round of cards face-up.
Each player looks at his own hole-card. The player with the highest upcard (nearest the dealer if there is a tie) either bets or folds. Other players in sequence from the left call, raise or fold. Another upcard is then dealt to each player still in the game, beginning with the player with the top pair of upcards, and another round of betting begins. A third upcard is dealt to the surviving players, and the player with the three best upcards opens the betting. Finally, a fourth upcard is dealt, and the round of betting is done on the same basis as before. After the final call, all hole cards are turned over and each player's whole hand exposed.

Six-Card Stud: In this version there is an additional deal added at the end, of a second face-down hole-card. But only five cards are produced for the showdown, leaving the player to decide which card to eliminate.

WHISKEY POKER **

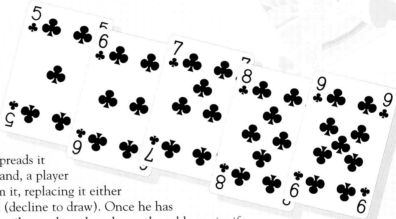

The players ante agreed and equal amounts into the pool. Dealer is chosen as for standard poker.
The dealer deals five cards to each player, with an extra Hand, the "widow" dealt face-down on the table. Eldest Hand starts play, and he may take up the widow and replace it with his own Hand, face-up, or refuse it. If he refuses, the choice passes to his left. If every player refuses the widow, then the dealer spreads it face-up on the table. Now, starting again with eldest Hand, a player can pick up the whole widow, or draw just one card from it, replacing it either with his own Hand or one card from his Hand, or stand (decline to draw). Once he has done so, or stood, the turn passes to his left, and so on until one player knocks on the table to signify he is happy with his Hand. The other players now have one more chance each, to draw or to stand. There are no bets or raises within the game, and it now goes straight to the showdown, in which each player shows his Hand. Scoring the Hands is as for standard poker, and the winner takes the pool.

PONTOON ✳✳✳

Also known in the USA as Blackjack, and in France as Vingt et Un (Twenty-One)

The Aim: To form a Hand whose total value is twenty-one, or which beats the dealer's.

Number of Players: From two to eight or more.

Scoring Values: Ace can be 1 or 11 at the player's choice; Kings, Queens, Jacks and 10's are all ten; other cards are at their pip value.

The Method: Use the standard 52-card pack (two packs shuffled together for eight or more players). Cut for banker (highest card; he is also the dealer). The banker deals one card to each player, starting on his left and ending with himself. His card remains face down; everyone else picks up their card. Starting from the banker's left, the players place their initial bets (between agreed maximum and minimum levels). The banker then deals a second card to each player, and now all the players including the banker look at their two cards. If the banker has a Pontoon (Ace - at 11 - plus a 10), he lays it down, face-up. Each player has to pay double their stake to the banker, and the round ends.

If the banker cannot declare a Pontoon, then each player, starting from his left has an opportunity to acquire extra cards. A player with a Pontoon declares it at this point by placing it on the table, the 10 face down and the Ace face-up on top of it. A player with two cards of equal value can split, by laying them face-up on the table and placing another stake equal to his first one. The banker deals another card, face-down, to each of these. If again there are equal-value cards, there can be a further split. Each of these hands may then be played, one after the other, during the player's turn.

Note: If the split cards are 10-point ones, they must be of the same nominal rank; two Jacks may be split but a Jack and a king cannot.

If a player's cards total under twenty-one, he can say "I'll buy one". He must bet again by the same amount as before, or up to double it, but not more. The banker then deals him another card. If his total is still under twenty-one, he can buy again, once again increasing his stake. This time he can raise it by any amount between the first bet and the second. If the total is still under twenty-one, he can buy and bet again, in the same way. Instead of buying, if his total is under twenty-one, a player can say "Twist". This means no increase in the stake, and the banker deals him another card. The player can then Twist again if his total is low, until he has up to five cards in his hand. Five cards totalling under twenty-one form a Five Card Trick (see next page). A player can buy and then twist, but not twist and then buy.

A player may decide to take no extra cards, and say "Stick". This is usual if his hand totals fifteen or more. Play then passes to the next player on the left. If at any time a player's hand exceeds twenty-one, he is "bust", and must throw in his hand, face-up, and lose his stake to the bank. A player who is bust on one split hand can still play the other.

When the players have completed their turns, the banker turns his two cards face-up. He can then add up to three extra cards, or stay with his hand. At the end of the round, after scoring is completed, there are several possibilities:

If no-one had a Pontoon, the dealer adds all the used cards to the bottom of the pack and deals again, without shuffling. If there was a Pontoon, the cards are shuffled and cut before the next deal. There is no change of banker unless he did not have a Pontoon, and another player did have one, without splitting his hand. That player then takes over the bank. If two or more players are eligible, then the one nearest the banker's left becomes the new banker.

A banker can also sell the bank to another player, after any round.

Scoring and Paying: If the banker has over twenty-one, he is bust. He pays their stakes back to all players who have not also gone bust, with double to anyone with a Pontoon or a Five Card Trick. If the banker has twenty-one or less, with not more than four cards, he pays their stake back to any player with a higher hand value, and collects from those with an equal or lower value. A banker who stayed on nineteen will say "Paying Twenty". All players then show their cards; those with twenty-one or a Five Card Trick receive double their stake. A banker with twenty-one pays on Pontoons and Five Card Tricks. If the banker has a Five Card Trick, he pays only Pontoons (double the stake).

Every other player, even those with Five Card Tricks, pay double their stake to the banker.

♣ RACING DEMON **

Number of Players: Two.

The Aim: To be first to get rid of your Demon pile, and to score 200 points.

The Method: Two 52-card packs are needed, with backs of different pattern or colour: one pack for each player. Aces are low. Each player deals thirteen cards face-down into a pile - these are the demon piles. The top card of each pile is turned over. Each player then deals a further four cards from his stock, placing them individually in a row to the right of the demon pile. These make the bases of foundation piles and can be built on in descending order of alternate colours (e.g. black 5, red 4, black 3, and so on). Cards can be added from the stock or from the turned-up top cards of the demon piles. Cards from the stock piles are turned up in sets of three: a card which cannot be used goes into a discard pile which becomes the stock once the original stock is exhausted. As Aces become available, they are placed face-up, separately, forming eight piles upon which either player can build in upwards sequence, treating the ace as low. Cards can be transferred to these piles but must then remain there. The aim is to get rid of the thirteen cards in your demon pile.

Scoring: The winner of a round scores 10. Each player scores one point for every card played (i. e. not in the demon pile, the stock or the discard pile). The player with cards left in his demon pile doubles their value and subtracts this from his total of played cards. If Kings are placed on the foundation piles, an extra ten points is awarded for each King.

♣ RED DOG *

Number of Players: Three can play, but the game is best with more than four.

The Aim: To take a chance on having a higher card than the top card of the stock pile.

The Method: Each player puts an agreed amount of chips or cash into the pool.

Use the standard 52-card pack. Cut for dealer (highest card). The dealer deals five cards to each player, or four if the number of players is nine or more. The remaining cards are placed face-down on the table, as the stock. The player to the dealer's left, having looked at his hand, bets anything from one chip to the whole pool that he holds a higher card of the same suit as the (unseen) top card on top of the stock. He must place his chips or coins alongside the pool. The dealer turns the top card over. If the player can produce a higher card of the same suit, then the dealer returns his stake and pays him from the pool. If the player loses, his bet goes into the pool and he shows his whole hand, face-up, after which it is discarded, and play passes to the next player on the left. A player can pass (not offer a bet) but must then pay one chip to the pool. If a player wins the whole pool, then each player contributes an equal amount to form a new pool and restart the game. If a player leaves the game, the pool must be equally divided and the game restarted.

RUMMY **

Number of Players: Two to six.

The Aim: To be the first player to "go out" by getting rid of all cards.

The Method: Use the standard 52-card pack. Aces are low. Cut for dealer (lowest card). Dealer deals cards according to the number of players: ten each to two players; seven each to three or four; six each to five or more. Cards are dealt out individually in rotation from the dealer's left. The rest of the pack is placed face down in the centre of the table, and the top card is turned face-up to start the discard pile. Having looked at his hand, the player on the dealer's left draws a card either from the top of the pack (unseen) or from the discard pile, and arranges his hand into melds of three or four, either by suit (consecutive, as 3-4-5-6), or by value (as three Kings). He places the melds, if any, face-down in front of him. Whether or not he lays down melds, he discards a single card face-up on the discard pile. This is the "upcard". The next player to the left does the same. He can also add cards to the melds already laid down ("laying off").

A player does not have to lay down his melds; he can retain them and hope to go out in a single turn.

This is to go rummy. The process continues round the players until one "goes out" by melding, laying off, or discarding his last card. If the whole pack is exhausted and no-one has gone out, the discard pile can be turned over, and the last upcard used to start a new discard pile.

Scoring: The player who goes out scores points for all the cards still held by his opponents: 10 for each court card, 1 for each Ace, others according to their pip value. A player who goes rummy gets double points.

Rummy can be, and often is, played as a gambling game rather than for points.

SERGEANT-MAJOR **

Number of Players: Three.

The Aim: To win the greatest number of tricks from a single hand.

The Method: Use the standard 52-card pack. Cut for dealer (highest card). The dealer deals 16 cards to each player. The last four cards are placed face-down, and form the kitty. The dealer chooses trumps. He then discards four of his cards, face-down, and picks up the kitty instead. The player to the dealer's left leads any card to the first trick. Other players must follow suit if they can, or trump, or discard. The trick is won by the highest card of the suit that led, or the highest trump. Each player has a target to meet. The dealer's is 8, the player's to his left is 5; the third player's is 3. At the end of the round, after scoring, the deal moves to the left. When the new deal is dealt, each player who was Up in the previous round gives away one card of his choice for each extra trick to a Down player, who must return the highest card he has of the same suit or suits. This can mean returning a card he has just been given. The game ends when any player wins 12 or more tricks from one hand.

Scoring: A player beating the target is said to Up by the difference between his score and the target; a player short of target is said to be Down by the same difference. Players who are Down pay one chip for each trick they are short by; players who are Up receive a chip for each extra trick.

SEVEN-UP **

Number of Players: Two to four, but two are best.

The Aim: To be first to reach seven points, by building up a trick-winning hand.

The Method: Use a standard 52-card pack. Aces are high. Draw for dealer - the higher card wins. Dealer deals six cards to each player, in two sets of three. The top card of the stock is then turned over to determine trumps. If a Jack is turned up, the dealer gets one point. The other player begins, by either standing (saying "I stand," and accepting the turned-up card as trumps) or begging (saying "I beg," and requesting a different suit). The dealer can accept or deny this request. If he accepts it, he deals three new cards to each and turns over the new top card of the stock, until a trump is agreed. If the dealer refuses to change trumps, the other player scores one point, and play continues. Each player, if necessary, discards enough cards to reduce his hand to six. The non-dealer leads, placing a card face-up. The dealer must follow suit, with a higher value, or play a trump to win the trick. Otherwise the trick goes to the other player. The winner of the trick leads the next card.

Scoring: Single points are won as follows:

High: The player dealt the highest trump in play

Low: The player dealt the lowest trump in play

Jack: The player winning the Jack of trumps in a trick (unless the dealer turned it over to determine trumps).

Game: The player with the highest total of point values for cards won in tricks. Values are: ace 4; King 3, Queen 2, Jack 1, ten 10. No other cards have any value. If only one trump card is played, it collects two points, or three if it is the Jack.

SKAT ***

Number of Players: Three.

The Aim: To be first to score ten game points.

The Method: Use a pack of 32 cards (Ace, King, Queen, Jack, 10, 9, 8, 7 in each suit). Cut for dealer (highest card). Dealer deals ten cards to each player, in sets of 3, then 4, then 3 at a time, and places the next two cards face-down on the table. These are the skat (also called the widow). The player to the dealer's left is First Hand. He has first right to pick up the skat. The player on his left (Middle Hand) is next if First Hand passes, and the third is Last Hand. He can pick up the skat if Middle Hand passes. The first player to take the skat is called the Player. He discards two cards face-down to replace the skat. The Player must make a contract to win at least 61 points in tricks taken (see trumps and point values). First Hand leads (he may or may not be the Player). Others must follow suit if they can; if not, they may play any card. A trick is won by the highest card of the suit led, or by the highest trump. The winner of the trick leads to the next trick. If all three players pass, the aim of the games changes. Now it is to win as few points in tricks as possible. The skat is set aside, and First Hand leads in the normal way. The skat is added to the cards of the player who wins the last trick. This variation of the game the game is called Least.

Trumps and Point Values: All Queens and Jacks and all Diamonds are trumps. This does not change. Ranking order of trumps is as follows: Queens of Clubs, Spades, Hearts, Diamonds; then Jacks in the same sequence of suits. Then come the other Diamonds: Ace, 10, King, 9, 8, 7. In the other suits, the ranking is: Ace, 10, King, 9, 8, 7. Note that the 10 outranks the King. Point values: Ace 11; 10 10; King 4; Queen 3; Jack 2; others: nil.

Scoring: 1. If the skat has been taken up: If the Player takes from 61 to 90 points (see Point Values) he scores two Game Points. If he takes 91 or more points, he scores four Game Points. This is called making Schneider. If he takes all the tricks he scores six Games Points (Schwartz). At the end of play, the point values of his two discards are also counted in his favour. If the Player falls short of his contract to win 61 or more points, he loses two Game Points if his score is between 31 and 60; and four Game Points (Schneider) if his score is under 31. If he takes no tricks at all, he loses six Game Points (Schwartz).

Scoring: 2. If the skat was not taken up: If a player has taken no tricks, he scores four Game Points. If a player has taken all the tricks, he loses four Game Points. If each player has taken at least one trick, the one with the lowest point value scores two Game Points. If two players tie with the same lowest point value, the two Game Points go to the player who lost the last trick between the two. If each player scores 40 value points, the dealer is awarded the two Game Points.

♣ SOLO **

Number of Players: Four.

The Aim: The highest bidder plays against the other three to take the number of tricks he bid for.

The Method: Use a standard 52-card pack. Aces are high. Cut for dealer (highest card). The dealer deals 13 cards to each player, from his left, in batches of 3,3,3,3,1. The final card is turned up in front of the dealer to propose the trump suit. Bidding begins with eldest hand, and goes to the left. Players can make a higher bid, or pass, or accept a Proposal. A player who has passed once may not bid again, and if a bid is followed by three consecutive passes, the bidder is the Soloist. Possible bids, in ascending order, are:

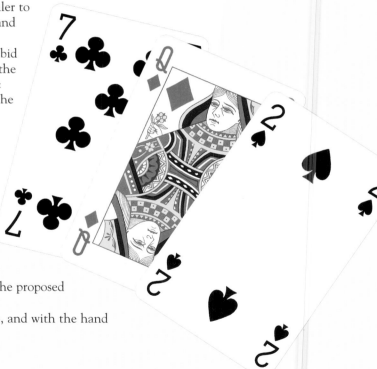

Proposal: a player says "I propose," or "Prop", if he thinks he and a partner can take at least eight tricks using the proposed trump suit. If no bid follows, another player may accept this proposal by saying "I accept," or "Cop". If no further bid is made, this bid stands and the two play as partners for the round. A higher bid cancels the Proposal.

Solo: a bid to take at least five tricks using the proposed trump suit.

Misere: a bid to take no tricks, playing at no trumps.

Abundance: a bid to win nine or more tricks using a trump suit named by the bidder.

Royal Abundance: a bid to win at least nine tricks using the proposed trump suit.

Spread Misere: a bid to win no tricks, playing at no trump, and with the hand placed face-up on the table after the first trick is played.

Abundance Declared: a bid to win all thirteen tricks, without a trump suit, but with the chance of leading to the first trick. This is the highest bid of all.

If eldest hand proposes and all others pass, he is able to raise his call to a Solo. If eldest hand passes, and another player proposes, without any higher call being made, eldest hand has the opportunity of accepting the proposal.

If all pass, the cards are thrown in and the deal passes to the left. Once the contract is made, the dealer takes the turned-up card into his hand and eldest hand leads, except in the case of Abundance Declared (unless he is also the soloist). Tricks are taken in the normal way: players must follow suit if possible; and the winner of the trick leads to the next.

Scoring: If the soloist makes his contract, he receives points from the other players; otherwise he pays points:

Proposal and Acceptance: 2 points

Solo: 2 points

Misere: 3 points

Abundance: (including Royal): 4 points

Spread Misere: 6 points

Abundance Declared: 8 points

In the case of Proposal/Acceptance, each of the partners receives or pays.

♣ SPOIL FIVE ***

Number of Players: Two to ten.

The Aim: To win three or five tricks, or to stop the other players from doing so, leaving the pool un-taken.

The Method: Use a standard pack of 52 cards. Each player puts an agreed number of tokens or coins in the pool.

One player deals until a Jack is dealt: the recipient of the Jack becomes dealer, reshuffles, and deals for the game. Hands of five are dealt, either 2 cards each and then 3, or vice versa. The top card of the stock is turned over to identify trumps. If it is an Ace, the dealer may immediately pick it up, and discard another card. If another player is holding the Ace of trumps, he passes a discard, face down, to the dealer, in exchange for the uncovered trump card.

If the dealer holds the ace of trumps, he discards under the stock, on his turn, and picks up the turned-up trump. Eldest hand makes the opening lead. Others must then follow suit or trump. If unable to follow suit, any card may be played but the trick will be lost. The trick is won by the highest card in the suit, or by the trump (higher card if trumps were led). The winner of the trick leads the next card. Reneging is possible: if a low trump is led, and the other player is holding the 5 or Jack of trumps, or the Ace of Hearts, he may retain these and play another card. But if a trump card higher than any of his is played, he must play the same suit. If no player wins three tricks, the game is "spoiled". The dealing switches to the next player on the left, more tokens go in the pool, and the game resumes.

If a player wins three tricks he wins the pool. If he takes the first three tricks in a row, he can either throw in his cards or say "Jink". This means he expects to win the two remaining tricks, and if he does so, the opponents pay him an extra token. If he fails, the pool stands and a new round begins.

Ranking structure in Spoil Five:

Whatever the trump suit, the Ace of Hearts is always the third-highest trump card.

Ranking of trumps otherwise starts with the 5 as highest card.

Hearts: 5, Jack, Ace, King, Queen, 10, 9, 8, 7,6, 4, 3, 2.

Diamonds: 5, Jack, Queen of Hearts, Ace, King, Queen,10, 9, 8, 7,6, 4, 3, 2.

Clubs and Spades: as with Diamonds.

In non-trump suits, the ranking is different for the red and black suits:

Hearts: Ace, King, Queen, Jack, 10, 9, 8,7, 6,5, 4, 3, 2.

Diamonds: As Hearts, but with Ace low.

Clubs and Spades: King, Queen, Jack, Ace, 2, 3, 4, 5, 6, 7, 8, 9, 10.

SWITCH *

Also played as Eights (see Note).

Number of Players: Two to eight.

The Aim: To be first to put down all your cards.

The Method: Use the standard 52-card pack, or two packs if there are six or more players. Cut for dealer (highest card). Dealer deals five cards to each player, one at a time, or seven cards if only two are playing.

The remaining cards are placed face-down to form the stock, and the top card is turned up and placed alongside the stock, as the starter.

If it is an Ace, replace it randomly in the stock pile and turn over the next card.

From the dealer's left, each player in turn plays a card on to the table, face-up, making a row from the starter card. Each card played must be of the same rank or the same suit as the previous one.

Aces are wild, and a player playing an ace can call a new suit to follow. It is not obligatory to play a card, but any player who does not, or cannot, must carry on drawing cards from the stock until he plays one. The game ends when one player has played all his cards; or if no-one can play a further card.

Scoring: Each opponent awards the winner points or payment relating to the value of the cards he is left holding. Aces are 50 points, all court cards 10, other cards by their pip value. If the game ends in a block, all players count their hands, and the player with the lowest total collects from each opponent the difference between his score and theirs.

Note: This game can also be played as Eights, when the eights are wild. The rules are the same, but in scoring, Aces count for 1 point and eights for 50. See also the game of Crazy Eights.

WHIST **

Number of Players: Four, playing as two sets of partners.

The Aim: To take more tricks than the opposing partnership.

The Method: Use the standard pack of 52. Normally two packs are employed, with different back designs, so that one may be shuffled while the other is being dealt. Aces are high.

Players draw cards to decide partners, who sit facing each other across the table. The draw can be decided according to either suit or value. A draw is also made to find the dealer (highest card, with aces low).

The dealer deals out thirteen cards to each player, one at a time, starting with the player to his left. The last card is turned face-up to determine trumps: the dealer then adds it to his hand.

The player to the dealer's left leads to the first trick. Others must follow suit if they can, otherwise trump or discard. The highest card of the led suit or a trump card wins.

One partner for each side takes charge of the side's won tricks. The winner of a trick leads to the next trick.

Scoring: A partnership, or pair, has to take at least seven tricks to score. The first six tricks won have no scoring value. After the seventh, each trick counts for one point. Revoking is penalised by three points. The first side to gain five points wins the game.

Points are also given for honour cards held. If a pair receive Ace, King, Queen and Jack of the trump suit (honour cards), they gain an extra four points. If they receive any three of the honour cards, they gain an extra two points. Points for honour cards are only given to a side which starts the deal with a score of less than four points.

Winning: Whist is normally played in a set of three games (a Rubber). The first side to win two games out of three wins the Rubber.

Note: The normal lead is the fourth card in your longest non-trump suit.

International Information

PERPETUAL CALENDAR

These charts enable you to find the day of the week in any year from 1754 throught 2032.

INSTRUCTIONS

STEP 1

Find the year that you are interested in below and note the letter that follows it.

STEP 2

Find that letter below and note which number falls under the month you are looking for.

STEP 3

Use the calendar that bears the number you found in step 2.

YEARS

	1788 I	1823 C	1858 E	1893 G	1928 N	1963 B	1998 D
1754 B	1789 D	1824 K	1859 F	1894 A	1929 B	1964 J	1999 E
1755 C	1790 E	1825 F	1860 N	1895 B	1930 C	1965 E	2000 M
1756 K	1791 F	1826 G	1861 B	1896 J	1931 D	1966 F	2001 A
1757 F	1792 N	1827 A	1862 C	1897 E	1932 L	1967 G	2002 B
1758 G	1793 B	1828 I	1863 D	1898 F	1933 G	1968 H	2003 C
1759 A	1794 C	1829 D	1864 L	1899 G	1934 A	1969 C	2004 K
1760 I	1795 D	1830 E	1865 G	1900 A	1935 B	1970 D	2005 F
1761 D	1796 L	1831 F	1866 A	1901 B	1936 J	1971 E	2006 G
1762 E	1797 G	1832 N	1867 B	1902 C	1937 E	1972 M	2007 A
1763 F	1798 A	1833 B	1868 J	1903 D	1938 F	1973 A	2008 I
1764 N	1799 B	1834 C	1869 E	1904 L	1939 G	1974 B	2009 D
1765 B	1800 C	1835 D	1870 F	1905 G	1940 H	1975 C	2010 E
1766 C	1801 D	1836 L	1871 G	1906 A	1941 C	1976 K	2011 F
1767 D	1802 E	1837 G	1872 H	1907 B	1942 D	1977 F	2012 N
1768 L	1803 F	1838 A	1873 C	1908 J	1943 E	1978 G	2013 B
1769 G	1804 N	1839 B	1874 D	1909 E	1944 M	1979 A	2014 C
1770 A	1805 B	1840 J	1875 E	1910 F	1945 A	1980 I	2015 D
1771 B	1806 C	1841 E	1876 M	1911 G	1946 B	1981 D	2016 L
1772 J	1807 D	1842 F	1877 A	1912 H	1947 C	1982 E	2017 G
1773 E	1808 L	1843 G	1878 B	1913 C	1948 K	1983 F	2018 A
1774 F	1809 G	1844 H	1879 C	1914 D	1949 F	1984 N	2019 B
1775 G	1810 A	1845 C	1880 K	1915 E	1950 G	1985 B	2020 J
1776 H	1811 B	1846 D	1881 F	1916 M	1951 A	1986 C	2021 E
1777 C	1812 J	1847 E	1882 G	1917 A	1952 I	1987 D	2022 F
1778 D	1813 E	1848 M	1883 A	1918 B	1953 E	1988 L	2023 G
1779 E	1814 F	1849 A	1884 I	1919 C	1954 E	1989 G	2024 H
1780 M	1815 G	1850 B	1885 D	1920 K	1955 F	1990 A	2025 C
1781 A	1816 H	1851 C	1886 E	1921 F	1956 N	1991 B	2026 D
1782 B	1817 C	1852 K	1887 F	1922 G	1957 B	1992 J	2027 E
1783 C	1818 D	1853 F	1888 B	1923 A	1958 C	1993 E	2028 M
1784 K	1819 E	1854 G	1889 B	1924 I	1959 D	1994 F	2029 A
1785 F	1820 M	1855 A	1890 C	1925 D	1960 L	1995 G	2030 B
1786 G	1821 A	1856 I	1891 D	1926 E	1961 G	1996 H	2031 C
1787 A	1822 B	1857 D	1892 L	1927 F	1962 A	1997 C	2032 K

MONTHS

	JAN	FEB	MAR	APR	MAY	JUN	JUL	AUG	SEP	OCT	NOV	DEC
A	1	4	4	7	2	5	7	3	6	1	4	6
B	2	5	5	1	3	6	1	4	7	2	5	7
C	3	6	6	2	4	7	2	5	1	3	6	1
D	4	7	7	3	5	1	3	6	2	4	7	2
E	5	1	1	4	6	2	4	7	3	5	1	3
F	6	2	2	5	7	3	5	1	4	6	2	4
G	7	3	3	6	1	4	6	2	5	7	3	5
H	1	4	5	1	3	6	1	4	7	2	5	7
I	2	5	6	2	4	7	2	5	1	3	6	1
J	3	6	7	3	5	1	3	6	2	4	7	2
K	4	7	1	4	6	2	4	7	3	5	1	3
L	5	1	2	5	7	3	5	1	4	6	2	4
M	6	2	3	6	1	4	6	2	5	7	3	5
N	7	3	4	7	2	5	7	3	6	1	4	6

CALENDARS

	1	2	3	4	5	6	7
Monday	1						
Tuesday	2	1					
Wednesday	3	2	1				
Thursday	4	3	2	1			
Friday	5	4	3	2	1		
Saturday	6	5	4	3	2	1	
Sunday	7	6	5	4	3	2	1
Monday	8	7	6	5	4	3	2
Tuesday	9	8	7	6	5	4	3
Wednesday	10	9	8	7	6	5	4
Thursday	11	10	9	8	7	6	5
Friday	12	11	10	9	8	7	6
Saturday	13	12	11	10	9	8	7
Sunday	14	13	12	11	10	9	8
Monday	15	14	13	12	11	10	9
Tuesday	16	15	14	13	12	11	10
Wednesday	17	16	15	14	13	12	11
Thursday	18	17	16	15	14	13	12
Friday	19	18	17	16	15	14	13
Saturday	20	19	18	17	16	15	14
Sunday	21	20	19	18	17	16	15
Monday	22	21	20	19	18	17	16
Tuesday	23	22	21	20	19	18	17
Wednesday	24	23	22	21	20	19	18
Thursday	25	24	23	22	21	20	19
Friday	26	25	24	23	22	21	20
Saturday	27	26	25	24	23	22	21
Sunday	28	27	26	25	24	23	22
Monday	29	28	27	26	25	24	23
Tuesday	30	29	28	27	26	25	24
Wednesday	31	30	29	28	27	26	25
Thursday		31	30	29	28	27	26
Friday			31	30	29	28	27
Saturday				31	30	29	28
Sunday					31	30	29
Monday						31	30
Tuesday							31

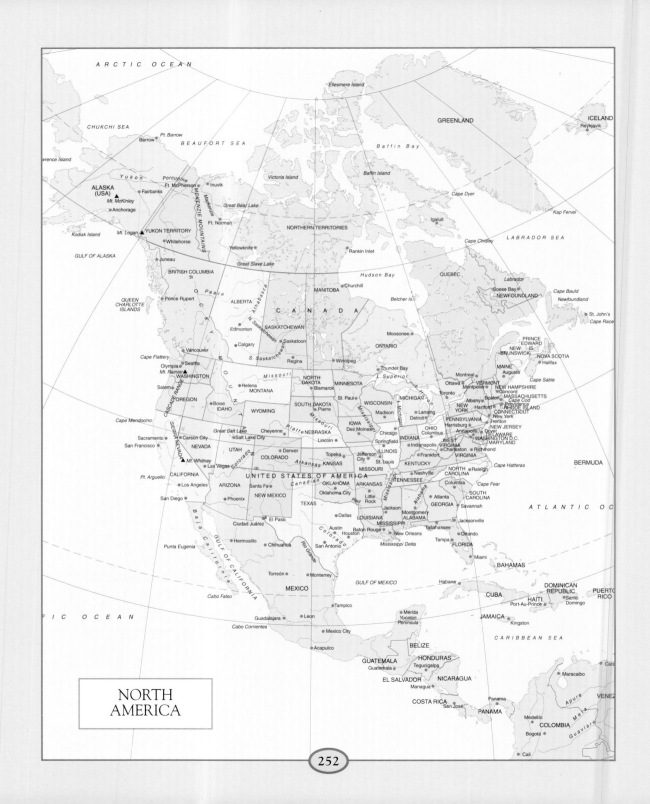

ARCTIC OCEAN

Ellesmere Island

CHUKCHI SEA

GREENLAND

ICELAND

Pt. Barrow

Reykjavik

Barrow

BEAUFORT SEA

Baffin Bay

wrence Island

Yukon

Porcupine

Victoria Island

Baffin Island

Ft. McPherson

ALASKA
(USA)

Inuvik

Cape Dyer

Fairbanks

MCKENZIE MOUNTAINS

Kap Fervel

Mt. McKinley

Mackenzie

Great Bear Lake

Anchorage

Ft. Norman

Kodiak Island

Mt. Logan

YUKON TERRITORY

NORTHERN TERRITORIES

LABRADOR SEA

Whitehorse

Yellowknife

Rankin Inlet

Cape Chidley

GULF OF ALASKA

Juneau

Great Slave Lake

Hudson Bay

QUEBEC

BRITISH COLUMBIA

Peace

Labrador

Churchill

Goose Bay

Cape Bauld

QUEEN
CHARLOTTE
ISLANDS

Prince Rupert

ALBERTA

N. Athabasca

Belcher Is.

NEWFOUNDLAND

Newfoundland

MANITOBA

ONTARIO

St. John's

Edmonton

SASKATCHEWAN

CANADA

Cape Race

Moosonee

S. Saskatchewan

PRINCE
EDWARD
IS.

Vancouver

Calgary

Saskatoon

NEW
BRUNSWICK

NOVA SCOTIA

Cape Flattery

Seattle

Regina

Winnipeg

Thunder Bay

Halifax

Olympia

Mt. Rainier

WASHINGTON

Missouri

Montreal

MAINE

Augusta

Cape Sable

Salem

OREGON

Helena

NORTH
DAKOTA

MINNESOTA

L. Superior

Toronto

Ottawa

VERMONT

Montpelier

NEW HAMPSHIRE

Concord

MASSACHUSETTS

Boise

MONTANA

Bismarck

St. Paul

WISCONSIN

MICHIGAN

Albany

Boston

Cape Cod

IDAHO

Madison

Lansing

NEW
YORK

Hartford

RHODE ISLAND

Providence

Cape Mendocino

WYOMING

SOUTH DAKOTA

Pierre

Detroit

OHIO

Trenton

New York

CONNECTICUT

Great Salt Lake

Cheyenne

Platte

Chicago

PENNSYLVANIA

NEW JERSEY

Sacramento

Carson City

Salt Lake City

NEBRASKA

IOWA

Des Moines

INDIANA

Harrisburg

DELAWARE

Dover

San Francisco

NEVADA

UTAH

Denver

Lincoln

Springfield

Indianapolis

Columbus

WASHINGTON D.C.

MARYLAND

COLORADO

Topeka

ILLINOIS

Frankfort

WEST
VIRGINIA

Annapolis

Richmond

Mt. Whitney

Las Vegas

Arkansas

KANSAS

Jefferson
City

St. Louis

MISSOURI

KENTUCKY

Nashville

VIRGINIA

BERMUDA

Pt. Arguello

CALIFORNIA

Santa Fe

OKLAHOMA

ARKANSAS

TENNESSEE

NORTH
CAROLINA

Raleigh

Cape Hatteras

Los Angeles

ARIZONA

NEW MEXICO

Oklahoma City

Little
Rock

Columbia

Cape Fear

San Diego

Phoenix

TEXAS

Canadian

Red

Atlanta

SOUTH
CAROLINA

Savannah

ATLANTIC OC

Dallas

Jackson

GEORGIA

Ciudad Juárez

El Paso

LOUISIANA

Montgomery

ALABAMA

Jacksonville

Hermosillo

Chihuahua

Colorado

Austin

MISSISSIPPI

Tallahassee

Orlando

Punta Eugenia

Baton Rouge

New Orleans

Tampa

FLORIDA

San Antonio

Houston

Mississippi Delta

Miami

Torreón

Monterrey

GULF OF MEXICO

BAHAMAS

FIC OCEAN

Cabo Falso

Tampico

Habana

DOMINICAN
REPUBLIC

PUERTO
RICO

Guadalajara

León

Mérida

CUBA

HAITI

Santo
Domingo

Cara

Yucatán
Peninsula

Port-Au-Prince

Cabo Corrientes

Mexico City

JAMAICA

Kingston

Acapulco

CARIBBEAN SEA

BELIZE

GUATEMALA

HONDURAS

Guatemala

Tegucigalpa

Maracaibo

EL SALVADOR

NICARAGUA

VENEZ

Managua

Panama

COSTA RICA

San José

PANAMA

Apure

Medellín

COLOMBIA

Mela

Bogotá

Guaviare

Cali

GULF OF CALIFORNIA

Baja California

Rio Grande

MEXICO

NORTH
AMERICA

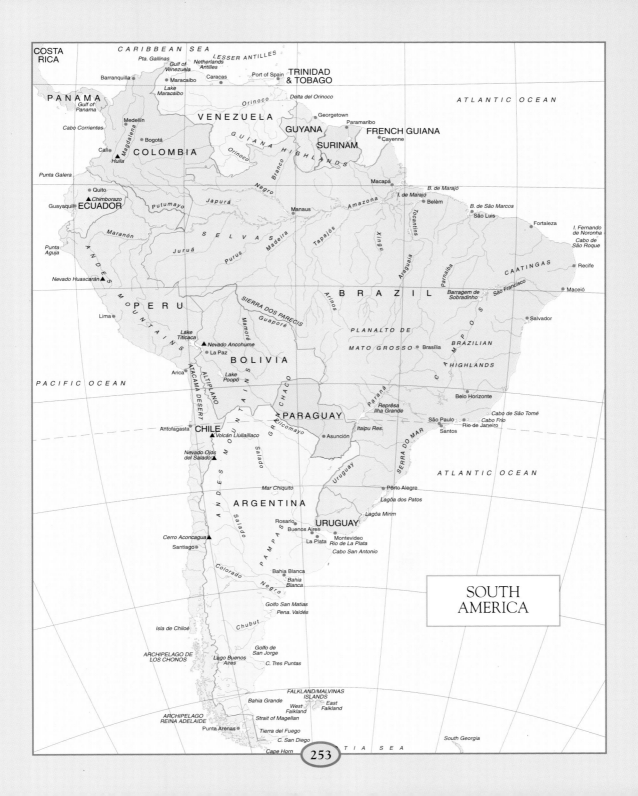

COSTA
RICA

CARIBBEAN SEA

Pta. Gallinas

LESSER ANTILLES

Netherlands
Antilles

Port of Spain

TRINIDAD
& TOBAGO

Barranquilla

Gulf of
Venezuela

Maracaibo

Caracas

PANAMA

Gulf of
Panama

Lake
Maracaibo

VENEZUELA

ATLANTIC OCEAN

Medellín

Cabo Corrientes

Bogotá

Georgetown

Orinoco

Delta del Orinoco

Paramaribo

GUYANA

SURINAM

FRENCH GUIANA

Cali

Huila ▲

COLOMBIA

G U I A N A

H I G H L A N D S

Cayenne

Punta Galera

Orinoco

Branco

Macapá

B. de Marajó

Quito

Negro

I. de Marajó

Belém

B. de São Marcos

Chimborazo ▲

ECUADOR

Japurá

São Luis

Guayaquil

Putumayo

Amazona

Manaus

Punta
Aguja

Marañón

Juruá

Purus

S E L V A S

Madeira

Tapajós

Xingu

Tocantins

Araguaia

Fortaleza

I. Fernando
de Noronha

Cabo de
São Roque

Nevado Huascarán ▲

A

N

D

E

S

Lima

PERU

M

O

U

N

T

A

I

N

S

SIERRA DOS PARECIS

Mamoré

Guaporé

B R A Z I L

Parnaíba

Recife

C A A T I N G A S

Barragem de
Sobradinho

São Francisco

Maceió

Lake
Titicaca

Nevado Ancohume ▲

La Paz

BOLIVIA

S E R R A

P L A N A L T O D E

M A T O G R O S S O

Brasília

B R A Z I L I A N

H I G H L A N D S

Salvador

M

Arica

ATACAMA

Lake
Poopó

DESERT

ALTIPLANO

A

N

D

E

S

G

R

A

N

C

H

A

C

O

Belo Horizonte

Antofagasta

CHILE

Volcán Llullaillaco ▲

M

O

U

N

T

A

I

N

S

Pilcomayo

PARAGUAY

Represa
Ilha Grande

Paraná

Itaipu Res.

Asunción

São Paulo

Cabo de São Tomé

Cabo Frio

Rio de Janeiro

Santos

Nevado Ojos
del Salado ▲

Salado

Uruguay

S E R R A D O M A R

ATLANTIC OCEAN

PACIFIC OCEAN

Mar Chiquito

ARGENTINA

Porto Alegre

Lagôa dos Patos

Lagôa Mirim

Cerro Aconcagua ▲

Salado

Rosario

Buenos Aires

URUGUAY

Santiago

P

A

M

P

A

S

La Plata

Montevideo

Rio de La Plata

Cabo San Antonio

Bahia Blanca

Colorado

Negro

Bahia
Blanca

Golfo San Matias

Pena. Valdés

Chubut

Isla de Chiloé

Golfo de
San Jorge

ARCHIPELAGO DE
LOS CHONOS

Lago Buenos
Aires

C. Tres Puntas

FALKLAND/MALVINAS
ISLANDS

Bahia Grande

West
Falkland

East
Falkland

ARCHIPELAGO
REINA ADELAIDE

Punta Arenas

Strait of Magellan

Tierra del Fuego

C. San Diego

South Georgia

Cape Horn

T I A S E A

SOUTH
AMERICA

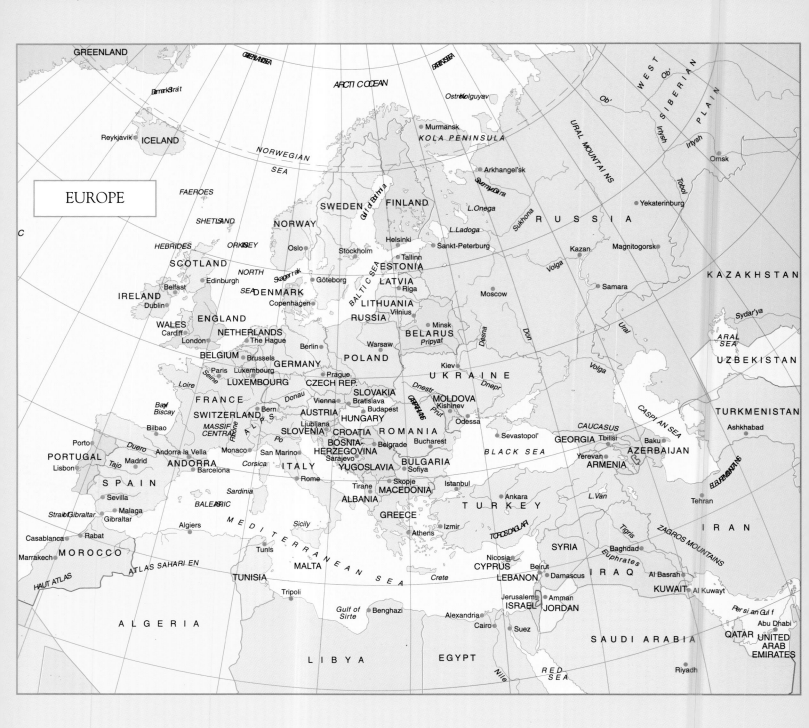

EUROPE

GREENLAND

ARCTIC OCEAN

Denmark Strait

Reykjavik ICELAND

NORWEGIAN SEA

FAEROES

SHETLAND

HEBRIDES ORKNEY

SCOTLAND

Belfast Edinburgh

IRELAND

Dublin

WALES ENGLAND
Cardiff
London

NETHERLANDS
The Hague

BELGIUM Brussels
Paris Luxembourg
LUXEMBOURG

FRANCE
Loire
Seine

Bay of Biscay

Bilbao

MASSIF CENTRAL

SWITZERLAND
Bern

Monaco

Porto

PORTUGAL Duero
Lisbon Tajo Madrid

ANDORRA
Andorra la Vella
Barcelona

SPAIN

Sevilla

Strait of Gibraltar
Gibraltar Malaga

Casablanca Rabat

MOROCCO

Marrakech

HAUT ATLAS

ATLAS SAHARIEN

ALGERIA

SWEDEN FINLAND

NORWAY

Oslo
Stockholm

Göteborg

NORTH SEA
DENMARK
Copenhagen

Skagerrak

Gulf of Bothnia

Helsinki

ESTONIA
Tallinn

BALTIC SEA
LATVIA
Riga

LITHUANIA
Vilnius

RUSSIA

Berlin
GERMANY
Prague
CZECH REP.

POLAND
Warsaw

BELARUS
Minsk

Pripyat

UKRAINE
Kiev

Murmansk

KOLA PENINSULA

L.Onega

L.Ladoga

Sankt-Peterburg

Moscow

Volga

Don

Deana

Dnepr

Arkhangel'sk

Severnaya Dvina

Sukhona

RUSSIA

Kazan

Volga

Ostrov Kolguyev

URAL MOUNTAINS

Yekaterinburg

Magnitogorsk

Samara

Ural

WEST SIBERIAN PLAIN

Ob'

Ob'

Irtysh

Irtysh

Tobol

Omsk

KAZAKHSTAN

Sydar'ya

ARAL SEA

UZBEKISTAN

SLOVAKIA
Bratislava
Vienna Budapest

AUSTRIA
Donau
Ljubljana
SLOVENIA
HUNGARY

ALPS

Rhone
Po
SAN MARINO

San Marino
Corsica

ITALY

Rome

Sardinia

BALEARIC

Algiers

Tunis

MEDITERRANEAN SEA

MALTA

TUNISIA

Tripoli

Gulf of Sirte
Benghazi

LIBYA

Sicily

CROATIA
BOSNIA-
HERZEGOVINA
Sarajevo
Belgrade

YUGOSLAVIA

Tirane
ALBANIA

ROMANIA
Bucharest

Dnestr

MOLDOVA
Kishinev

Prut

Odessa

Sevastopol'

BLACK SEA

BULGARIA
Sofiya

Skopje
MACEDONIA

GREECE

Athens

Crete

Istanbul

Izmir

Ankara

L.Van

TOROS DAGLARI

Nicosia
CYPRUS

Beirut
LEBANON

Jerusalem
ISRAEL

Amman
JORDAN

Damascus

SYRIA
Baghdad

IRAQ
Euphrates

Al Basrah

KUWAIT
Al Kuwayt

Alexandria

Cairo

Suez

EGYPT

Nile

RED SEA

SAUDI ARABIA

Riyadh

Carpathians

GEORGIA
Tbilisi

CAUCASUS

ARMENIA
Yerevan

Baku

CASPIAN SEA

AZERBAIJAN

TURKMENISTAN

Ashkhabad

ELBURZ MOUNTAINS

Tehran

ZAGROS MOUNTAINS

IRAN

Tigris

Persian Gulf

Abu Dhabi

QATAR

UNITED ARAB EMIRATES

TURKEY

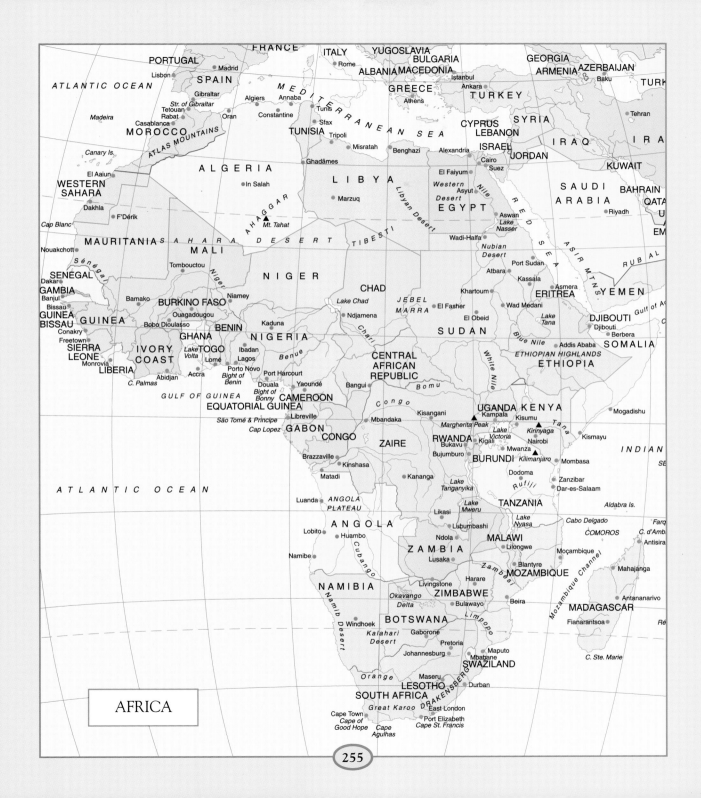

AFRICA

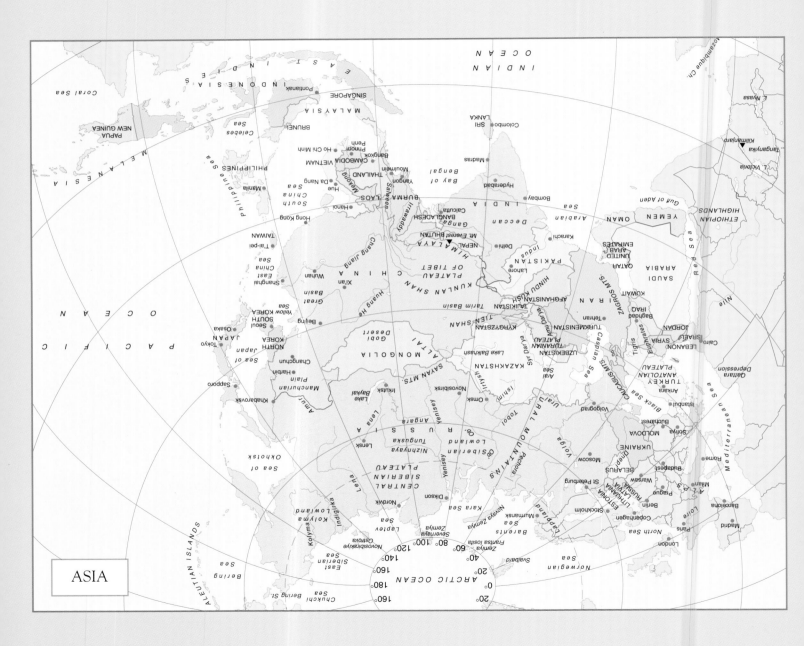

ASIA

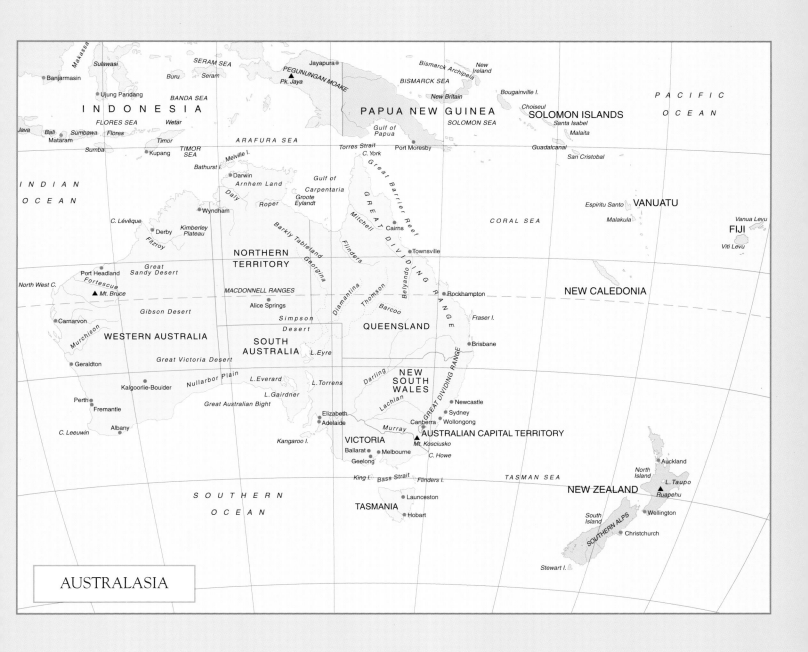

Makassar
Sulawesi
SERAM SEA
Jayapura
Bismarck Archipelago
New Ireland
PACIFIC
Banjarmasin
Buru
Seram
PEGUNUNGAN MOAKE
BISMARCK SEA
OCEAN
Ujung Pandang
BANDA SEA
Pk. Jaya
New Britain
Bougainville I.
INDONESIA
FLORES SEA
Wetar
PAPUA NEW GUINEA
SOLOMON ISLANDS
Choiseul
Santa Isabel
Java
Bali
Sumbawa
Flores
Gulf of
SOLOMON SEA
Malaita
Mataram
Papua
Sumba
Timor
ARAFURA SEA
Torres Strait
Port Moresby
Guadalcanal
Kupang
TIMOR
C. York
San Cristobal
SEA
Melville I.
INDIAN
Bathurst I.
Darwin
Gulf of
OCEAN
Daly
Arnhem Land
Carpentaria
VANUATU
Wyndham
Roper
Groote
Espiritu Santo
C. Lévêque
Eylandt
Cairns
Malakula
Vanua Levu
Derby
Kimberley
Barkly Tableland
CORAL SEA
FIJI
Fitzroy
Plateau
NORTHERN
Townsville
Viti Levu
Port Headland
TERRITORY
Fortescue
Great
Georgina
NEW CALEDONIA
Sandy Desert
Rockhampton
Mt. Bruce
MACDONNELL RANGES
Carnarvon
Gibson Desert
Alice Springs
Thomson
Fraser I.
Simpson
Barcoo
Murchison
WESTERN AUSTRALIA
Desert
QUEENSLAND
Geraldton
SOUTH
L. Eyre
Brisbane
Great Victoria Desert
AUSTRALIA
Kalgoorlie-Boulder
Nullarbor Plain
L. Everard
L. Torrens
NEW
Newcastle
Perth
L. Gairdner
Darling
SOUTH
Sydney
Fremantle
Great Australian Bight
Lachlan
WALES
Wollongong
Elizabeth
Canberra
AUSTRALIAN CAPITAL TERRITORY
C. Leeuwin
Albany
Adelaide
Murray
Kangaroo I.
VICTORIA
Mt. Kosciusko
Auckland
Ballarat
C. Howe
North
Geelong
Melbourne
Island
L. Taupo
King I.
Bass Strait
Flinders I.
TASMAN SEA
Ruapehu
SOUTHERN
Launceston
NEW ZEALAND
Wellington
OCEAN
TASMANIA
South
SOUTHERN ALPS
Hobart
Island
Christchurch
Stewart I.

AUSTRALASIA

THE NORTH POLE

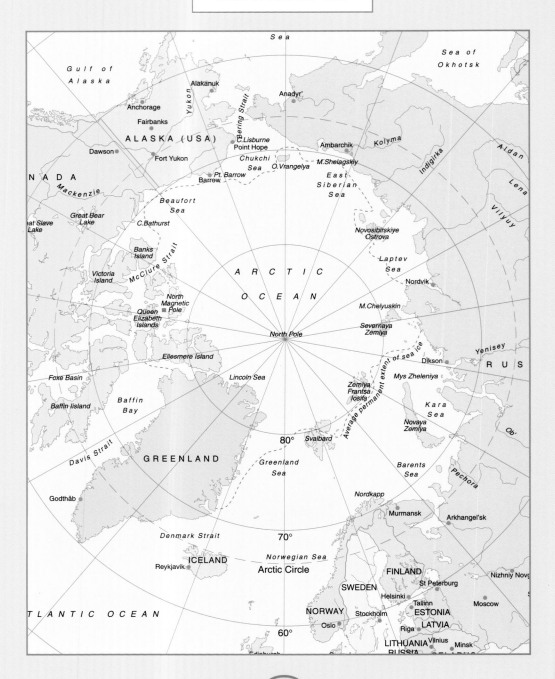

Sea

Gulf of
Alaska

Sea of
Okhotsk

Alakanuk

Anchorage

Anadyr'

Fairbanks

Yukon

ALASKA (USA)

C.Lisburne
Point Hope

Ambarchik

Kolyma

Aldan

Dawson

Fort Yukon

Chukchi
Sea

O.Vrangelya

M.Shelagskiy

Indigirka

Lena

NADA

Pt. Barrow
Barrow

East
Siberian
Sea

Vilyuy

Mackenzie

Beaufort
Sea

Great Bear
Lake

eat Slave
Lake

C.Bathurst

Novosibirskiye
Ostrova

Banks
Island

McClure Strait

Laptev
Sea

Victoria
Island

A R C T I C

O C E A N

Nordvik

North
Magnetic
Pole

M.Cheluyskin

Queen
Elizabeth
Islands

North Pole

Severnaya
Zemlya

Ellesmere Island

Yenisey

R U S

Lincoln Sea

Dikson

Foxe Basin

Zemlya
Frantsa
Iosifa

Mys Zheleniya

Baffin lisland

Baffin
Bay

Kara
Sea

Ob'

Novaya
Zemlya

80°

Svalbard

Davis Strait

GREENLAND

Greenland
Sea

Barents
Sea

Pechora

70°

Nordkapp

Godthåb

Murmansk

Arkhangel'sk

Denmark Strait

ICELAND

Norwegian Sea

Arctic Circle

FINLAND

Nizhniy Novg

Reykjavik

St Peterburg

SWEDEN

Helsinki

Moscow

NORWAY

Tallinn

Estonia

60°

Oslo

Stockholm

LATVIA

Riga

LITHUANIA

Vilnius

Minsk

RUSSIA

Average permanent extent of sea ice

THE SOUTH POLE

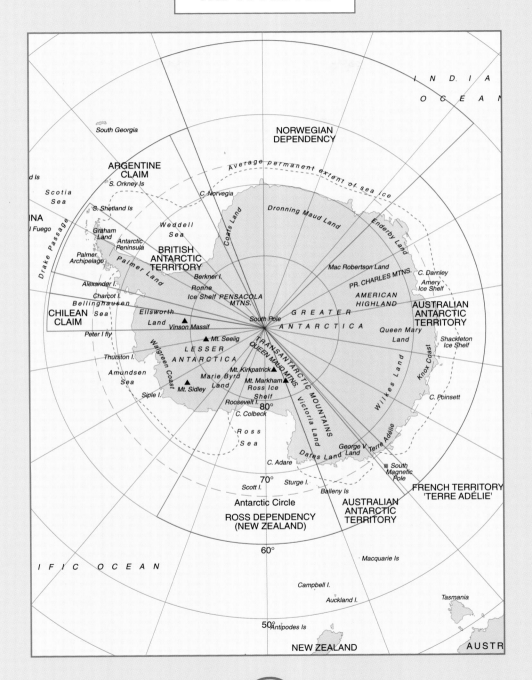

INDIA OCEAN

South Georgia

NORWEGIAN DEPENDENCY

ARGENTINE CLAIM

S. Orkney Is

Average permanent extent of sea ice

Scotia Sea

Dronning Maud Land

Enderby Land

S. Shetland Is

C. Norvegia

NA

Weddell Sea

Coats Land

Mac Robertson Land

C. Darnley

Fuego

d Is

Drake Passage

Graham Land

Antarctic Peninsula

BRITISH ANTARCTIC TERRITORY

Berkner I.

PR. CHARLES MTNS.

Amery Ice Shelf

Palmer Archipelago

Palmer Land

Ronne Ice Shelf

PENSACOLA MTNS.

AMERICAN HIGHLAND

AUSTRALIAN ANTARCTIC TERRITORY

Alexander I.

Charcot I.

GREATER ANTARCTICA

Bellinghausen Sea

CHILEAN CLAIM

Ellsworth Land

South Pole

Queen Mary Land

Shackleton Ice Shelf

Vinson Massif

Peter I Isly

Mt. Seelig

TRANSANTARCTIC QUEEN MAUD MTNS.

Knox Coast

Thurston I.

LESSER ANTARCTICA

MOUNTAINS

Wilkes Land

C. Poinsett

Amundsen Sea

Walgreen Coast

Mt. Kirkpatrick

Marie Byrd Land

Mt. Markham

MOUNTAINS

Victoria Land

Siple I.

Mt. Sidley

Ross Ice Shelf

Roosevelt I.

80°

C. Colbeck

Terre Adélie

Ross Sea

South Magnetic Pole

C. Adare

George V Land

Dates Land

70°

Sturge I.

FRENCH TERRITORY 'TERRE ADÉLIE'

Scott I.

Balleny Is

Antarctic Circle

ROSS DEPENDENCY (NEW ZEALAND)

AUSTRALIAN ANTARCTIC TERRITORY

60°

Macquarie Is

IFIC OCEAN

Campbell I.

Auckland I.

Tasmania

50°

Antipodes Is

NEW ZEALAND

AUSTR

CLIMATE IN SELECTED WORLD CITIES

Temperatures are given in degrees Fahrenheit; precipitation in inches.

CITY & COUNTRY	AVERAGE DAILY TEMPERATURE								AVERAGE PRECIPITATION												
	JANUARY		APRIL		JULY		OCTOBER		JANUARY	FEBRUARY	MARCH	APRIL	MAY	JUNE	JULY	AUGUST	SEPTEMBER	OCTOBER	NOVEMBER	DECEMBER	YEAR TOTAL
	MAXIMUM	MINIMUM	MAXIMUM	MINIMUM	MAXIMUM	MINIMUM	MAXIMUM	MINIMUM													
Algiers, Algeria	59	49	68	55	83	70	74	63	4.4	3.3	2.9	1.6	1.8	0.6	0.0	0.2	1.6	3.1	5.1	5.4	30.0
Ankara, Turkey	39	24	63	40	86	59	69	44	1.3	1.2	1.3	1.3	1.9	1.0	0.5	0.4	0.7	0.6	1.2	1.9	13.3
Athens, Greece	55	44	68	52	92	73	75	60	2.4	1.5	1.5	1.0	1.0	0.6	0.2	0.3	0.6	2.0	2.2	2.8	16.1
Belgrade, Serbia	37	26	64	45	83	62	64	47	1.9	1.8	1.8	2.1	2.9	3.8	2.4	2.2	2.0	2.2	2.4	2.2	27.7
Buenos Aires, Argentina	85	63	72	53	57	42	69	50	3.1	2.8	4.3	3.5	3.0	2.4	2.2	2.4	3.1	3.4	3.3	3.9	37.4
Canberra, Australia	82	55	67	44	52	33	68	43	1.9	1.7	2.2	1.6	1.8	2.1	1.8	2.2	1.6	2.2	1.9	2.0	23.0
Caracas, Venezuela	75	56	81	60	78	61	79	61	0.9	0.4	0.6	1.3	3.1	4.0	4.3	4.3	4.2	4.3	3.7	1.8	32.9
Copenhagen, Denmark	36	28	51	38	71	57	54	44	1.9	1.5	1.3	1.5	1.7	1.9	2.8	2.6	2.4	2.3	1.9	1.9	23.7
Dakar, Senegal	79	64	81	65	88	76	89	76	0.0	0.0	0.0	0.0	0.0	0.7	3.5	10.0	5.2	1.5	0.1	0.3	21.3
DeBilt, Netherlands	40	31	56	40	72	55	57	44	2.7	2.1	1.7	1.9	2.1	2.3	3.0	3.4	2.8	2.8	2.8	2.5	30.1
Dehli, India	70	44	97	68	96	81	93	65	0.9	0.7	0.5	0.3	0.5	2.9	7.1	6.8	4.6	0.4	0.1	0.4	25.2
Dublin, Ireland	46	34	55	39	67	52	57	43	2.6	2.2	2.0	1.8	2.4	2.2	2.8	2.9	2.8	2.8	2.6	2.9	30.0
Frankfurt, Germany	38	29	60	42	77	58	58	44	2.3	1.7	1.5	1.7	2.2	2.9	2.8	3.0	2.2	2.1	2.2	2.1	26.7
Godthaab, Greenland	19	10	31	20	52	38	35	26	1.4	1.7	1.6	1.2	1.7	1.4	2.2	3.1	3.3	2.5	1.9	1.5	23.5
Hamilton, Bermuda	68	58	71	59	85	73	79	69	4.4	4.7	4.8	4.1	4.6	4.4	4.5	5.4	5.2	5.8	5.0	4.7	57.6
Harare, Zimbabwe	78	60	78	55	70	44	83	58	7.7	7.0	4.6	1.1	0.5	0.1	0.0	0.1	0.2	1.1	3.8	6.4	32.6
Helsinki, Finland	26	17	44	30	71	55	47	37	2.2	1.7	1.4	1.7	1.6	2.0	2.7	2.8	2.8	2.9	2.7	2.6	27.1
Hong Kong	64	56	75	67	87	78	81	73	1.3	1.8	2.9	5.4	11.5	15.5	15.0	14.2	10.1	4.5	1.7	1.2	85.1
Jakarta, Indonesia	84	74	87	75	87	73	87	74	11.8	11.8	8.3	5.8	4.5	3.8	2.5	1.7	2.6	4.4	5.6	8.0	70.8
Jerusalem, Israel	55	41	73	50	87	63	81	59	5.2	5.2	2.5	1.1	0.1	0.0	0.0	0.0	0.0	0.5	2.8	3.4	20.8
Karachi, Pakistan	77	55	90	73	91	81	91	72	0.5	0.4	0.3	0.1	0.1	0.7	3.2	1.6	0.5	0.0	0.1	0.2	7.7
Kinshasa, Zaire	87	70	89	71	81	64	88	70	5.3	5.7	7.7	7.7	6.2	0.3	0.1	0.1	1.2	4.7	8.7	5.6	53.3
Lisbon, Portugal	57	46	67	53	81	63	72	58	4.3	3.0	4.2	2.1	1.7	0.6	0.1	0.2	1.3	2.4	3.7	4.1	27.7
London, United Kingdom	43	36	56	42	71	56	58	46	21	1.6	1.5	1.5	1.8	1.8	2.2	2.3	1.9	2.2	2.5	1.9	23.3
Madrid, Spain	47	35	65	45	87	63	65	49	1.5	1.3	1.7	1.9	1.9	1.0	0.4	0.6	1.3	2.1	1.9	1.9	17.5
Manila, Philippines	86	69	93	73	88	75	88	74	0.9	0.5	0.7	1.3	5.1	10.0	17.0	16.6	14.0	7.6	5.7	2.6	82.0
Mexico City, Mexico	66	42	77	51	73	53	70	50	0.5	0.2	0.4	0.8	2.1	4.7	6.7	6.0	5.1	2.0	0.7	0.3	29.5
Monte Carlo, Monaco	54	47	61	54	78	71	68	61	2.4	2.3	2.8	2.6	2.5	1.3	0.8	0.9	2.6	4.5	4.8	3.9	31.4
Moscow, Russia	15	3	50	34	73	55	48	37	1.5	1.5	1.4	1.5	2.1	2.3	3.5	2.8	2.3	1.8	1.9	2.1	24.7
Nairobi, Kenya	77	54	75	58	69	51	76	55	1.5	2.5	4.9	8.3	6.2	1.8	0.6	0.9	1.2	2.1	4.3	3.4	37.7
Nassau, Bahamas	77	65	81	69	88	75	85	73	1.4	1.5	1.4	2.5	4.6	6.4	5.8	5.3	6.9	6.5	2.8	1.3	46.4
Oslo, Norway	28	19	50	34	72	55	48	38	1.9	1.4	1.0	1.7	1.7	2.8	3.2	3.7	3.2	2.9	2.7	2.5	28.7
Ottawa, Canada	21	3	51	31	81	58	54	37	2.9	2.2	2.8	2.7	2.5	3.5	3.4	2.6	3.2	2.9	3.0	2.6	34.3
Paris, France	43	34	60	43	76	58	60	46	2.2	1.8	1.4	1.7	2.2	2.1	2.3	2.5	2.2	2.0	2.0	2.0	24.4
Port Moresby, Papua New Guinea	89	76	87	75	83	73	86	75	7.0	7.6	6.7	4.2	2.5	1.3	1.1	0.7	1.0	1.4	1.9	4.4	39.8
Reykjavik, Iceland	35	28	43	33	57	48	45	38	3.5	2.5	2.4	2.2	1.7	1.7	2.0	2.2	2.6	3.7	3.1	3.1	30.7
Rio de Janeiro, Brazil	84	73	80	69	75	63	77	66	4.9	4.8	5.1	4.2	3.1	2.1	1.6	1.7	2.6	3.1	4.1	5.4	42.7
Riyadh, Saudi Arabia	70	46	89	64	107	78	94	61	0.1	0.8	0.9	1.0	0.4	0.0	0.0	0.0	0.0	0.0	0.0	0.0	3.2
Rome, Italy	52	40	66	50	87	67	71	55	2.8	2.4	2.2	2.0	1.8	1.5	0.6	0.8	2.5	3.9	5.9	3.7	30.1
San Jose, Costa Rica	75	58	79	62	77	62	77	60	0.6	0.2	0.8	1.8	9.0	9.5	8.3	9.5	12.0	11.8	5.7	1.6	70.8
Shanghai, China	46	33	66	50	90	74	74	57	1.9	2.3	3.3	3.7	3.7	7.1	5.8	5.6	5.1	2.8	2.0	1.4	44.7
Singapore	86	73	88	75	88	75	87	74	9.9	6.8	7.6	7.4	6.8	6.8	6.7	7.7	7.0	8.2	10.0	10.1	95.0
Stockholm, Sweden	30	23	47	34	71	57	49	41	1.7	1.2	1.0	1.2	1.3	1.8	2.4	3.0	2.4	1.9	2.1	1.9	21.9
Tokyo, Japan	47	29	63	46	83	70	69	55	1.9	2.9	4.2	5.3	5.8	6..5	5.6	6.0	9.2	8.2	3.8	2.2	61.6
Vienna, Austria	34	25	58	42	76	60	56	44	1.5	1.7	1.7	1.8	2.8	2.6	3.3	2.8	1.7	2.2	2.1	1.8	26.0
Warsaw, Poland	32	22	53	37	75	58	55	41	1.1	1.3	1.1	1.5	1.8	2.7	3.8	2.6	1.7	1.5	1.2	1.7	22.0
Wellington, New Zealand	69	56	63	51	53	42	60	48	3.2	3.2	3.2	3.8	4.6	4.6	5.4	4.6	3.8	4.0	3.5	3.5	47.4
Zurich, Switzerland	36	26	59	40	76	56	57	43	2.9	2.7	2.5	3.0	4.0	5.1	5.4	4.9	4.0	3.0	2.9	2.5	42.9

	Amsterdam	Atlanta	Bangkok	Boston	Charlotte	Chicago	Dallas/Ft. Worth	Denver	Detroit	Frankfurt	Hong Kong	Honolulu	Houston	Las Vegas	London	Los Angeles
Amsterdam	...	4387	5699	3447	4184	4110	4906	4814	3926	227	5769	7238	4999	5356	230	5561
Atlanta	4387	...	9170	945	225	606	729	1201	596	4600	8389	4501	688	1746	4198	1940
Bangkok	5699	9170	...	8507	9076	8573	8993	8422	8594	5570	1067	6580	9284	8275	5928	7702
Boston	3447	945	8507	...	727	864	1561	1748	631	3658	7949	5082	1595	2381	3255	2603
Charlotte	4184	225	9076	727	...	599	936	1340	500	4388	8347	4678	918	1716	3980	2118
Chicago	4110	606	8573	864	599	...	802	885	234	4329	7783	4233	926	1510	3941	1740
Dallas/Ft. Worth	4906	729	8993	1561	936	802	...	641	973	5127	8096	3776	224	1052	4736	1231
Denver	4814	1201	8422	1748	1340	885	641	...	1119	5041	7477	862	457	627	4655	864
Detroit	3926	596	8594	631	500	234	973	1119	...	4146	7831	4464	1075	1749	3754	1973
Frankfurt	227	4600	5570	3658	4388	4329	5127	5041	4146	...	5695	7432	5218	5584	407	5787
Hong Kong	5769	8389	1067	7949	8347	7783	8096	7477	7831	5695	...	5538	8334	7288	5990	7230
Honolulu	7238	4501	6580	5082	4678	4233	3776	862	4464	7432	5538	...	3895	2758	7220	2551
Houston	4999	688	9284	1595	918	926	224	457	1075	5218	8339	3895	...	1233	4821	1374
Las Vegas	5356	1746	8275	2381	1916	1510	1052	627	1749	5584	7288	2758	1233	...	5230	235
London	230	4198	5928	3255	3980	3941	4736	4655	3754	407	5990	7220	4821	5230	...	5439
Los Angeles	5561	1940	7702	2603	2118	1740	1231	864	1973	5787	7230	2551	1374	235	5439	...
Madrid	906	4351	6311	3398	4109	4188	4966	5023	3979	882	6536	7853	5018	5612	773	5846
Miami	4621	595	9635	1260	651	1198	1119	1711	1147	4820	8968	4862	963	2174	4414	2336
Minn./St. Paul	4151	906	8289	1120	930	333	852	682	527	4202	7475	3964	1035	1296	4001	1532
New York	3630	760	8644	186	540	738	1387	1620	508	3844	8050	4972	1415	2241	3440	2467
Orlando	4540	405	9461	1122	468	1006	966	1547	957	4745	8780	4753	852	2038	4321	2211
Paris	247	4382	5848	3436	4173	4138	4932	4863	3949	279	5966	7424	5012	5443	215	5652
Philadelphia	3725	665	8705	279	447	677	1299	1553	454	3935	8090	4908	1323	2176	3533	2395
Phoenix	5410	1587	8526	2294	1774	1437	877	602	1666	5637	7543	2911	1006	255	5256	368
Pittsburgh	3894	525	8677	483	366	429	1067	1292	202	4120	8009	4658	1124	1910	3702	2146
Rome	804	5035	5439	4077	4811	4806	5614	5545	4612	594	5776	8023	5696	6127	895	6335
St. Louis	4370	484	8728	1043	575	258	545	767	438	4593	7939	4120	668	1367	4187	1587
Salt Lake city	4990	1589	8129	2105	1727	1246	989	391	1489	5218	7178	2989	1193	367	4850	589
San Francisco	5454	2133	7910	2695	2296	1841	1460	970	2073	5680	6896	2394	1631	413	5351	339
Seattle	4887	2176	7435	2496	2279	1715	1656	1028	1912	5109	6473	2672	1871	886	4784	955
Seoul	5316	7138	2290	6820	7118	6519	6806	6188	6620	5312	1291	4545	7069	6003	5507	5959
Singapore	6527	9865	897	9365	9806	9345	9698	9050	9352	6382	1601	6699	9856	8822	6756	8766
Sydney	10,342	9252	4684	9978	9457	9228	8575	8343	9429	10,242	4582	5073	8582	7719	10,568	7489
Tokyo	5784	6832	2868	6709	6898	6287	6410	5789	6423	5812	1797	3846	6665	5515	5955	5473
Toronto	3721	740	8451	445	589	435	1197	1310	213	3939	7788	4638	1280	1937	3544	2170

Madrid	Miami	Minn./St. Paul	New York	Orlando	Paris	Philadelphia	Phoenix	Pittsburgh	Rome	St. Louis	Salt Lake City	San Francisco	Seattle	Seoul	Singapore	Sydney	Tokyo	Toronto
906	4621	4151	3630	4540	247	3725	5410	3894	804	4370	4990	5454	4887	5316	6527	10,342	5784	3721
4351	595	906	760	405	4382	665	1587	525	5035	484	1589	2133	2176	7138	9865	9252	6832	740
6311	9635	8289	8644	9461	5848	8705	8526	8677	5493	8728	8129	7910	7435	2290	897	4684	2868	8451
3398	1260	1120	186	1122	3436	279	2294	483	4077	1043	2105	2695	2496	6820	9365	9978	6709	445
4109	651	930	540	468	4173	447	1774	366	4811	575	1727	2296	2279	7118	9806	9457	6898	589
4188	1198	333	738	1006	4138	677	1437	429	4806	258	1246	1841	1715	6519	9345	9228	6287	435
4966	1119	852	1387	966	4932	1299	877	1067	5614	545	986	1460	1656	6806	9698	8575	6410	1197
5023	1711	682	1620	1547	4863	1553	602	1292	5545	767	391	970	1028	6188	9050	8343	5789	1310
3979	1147	527	508	957	3949	454	1666	202	4612	438	1489	2073	1912	6620	9352	9429	6423	213
882	4820	4202	3844	4745	279	3935	5637	4120	594	4593	5218	5680	5109	5312	6382	10,242	5812	3939
6536	8968	7475	8050	8780	5966	8090	7543	8009	5776	7939	7178	6896	6473	1291	1601	4582	1797	7788
7853	4862	3964	4972	4753	7424	4908	2911	4658	8023	4120	2989	2394	2672	4545	6699	5073	3846	4638
5018	963	1035	1415	852	5012	1323	1006	1124	5696	668	1193	1631	1871	7069	9856	8582	6665	1280
5612	2174	1296	2241	2038	5443	2176	255	1910	6127	1367	367	413	866	6003	8822	7719	5515	1937
773	4414	4001	3440	4321	215	3533	5256	3702	895	4187	4850	5351	4784	5507	6756	10,568	5955	3544
5846	2336	1532	2467	2211	5652	2395	368	2146	6335	1587	589	339	955	5959	8766	7489	5473	2170
...	4412	4332	3578	4375	661	3671	5608	3900	826	4428	5263	5812	5311	6194	7067	10,974	6687	3764
4412	...	1501	1091	193	4574	1015	1972	1004	5171	1069	2088	2580	2817	7732	10,330	9300	7451	1235
4332	1501	...	1025	1310	4222	977	1275	726	4902	448	988	1585	1394	6234	9055	8985	5963	676
4332	1091	1025	...	937	3622	93	2177	324	4263	889	1983	2578	2413	6874	9525	9944	6754	366
4375	193	1310	937	...	4495	861	1847	834	5112	880	1929	2445	2553	7533	10,179	9310	7252	1057
661	4574	4222	3622	4495	...	3715	5487	3910	683	4398	5080	5592	5017	5549	6658	10,520	6027	3738
3671	1015	977	93	861	3715	...	2075	250	4357	811	1926	2514	2370	6925	9538	9782	6765	347
5608	1972	1275	2177	1847	5487	2075	...	1813	6164	1259	508	650	1106	6259	9067	7797	5768	1871
3900	1004	726	324	834	3910	250	1813	...	4550	566	5118	2265	2124	6795	9487	9553	6587	222
826	5171	4902	4263	5115	683	4357	6164	4550	...	5065	5764	6246	5688	5575	6240	10,147	6143	4399
4428	1069	448	889	880	4398	811	1259	566	5065	...	1152	1731	1704	6675	9476	9036	6398	653
5263	2088	988	1983	1929	5080	1926	508	5118	5764	1152	...	598	688	5888	8747	8012	5455	1654
5812	2580	1585	2578	2445	5592	2514	650	2265	6246	1731	598	...	678	5615	8438	7420	5145	2253
5311	2817	1394	2413	2553	5017	2370	1106	2124	5688	1704	688	678	...	5183	8068	7740	4790	2037
6194	7732	6234	6874	7533	5549	6925	6259	6795	5575	6675	5888	5615	5183	...	2888	5178	732	6601
7067	10,330	9055	9525	10,179	6658	9538	9067	9487	6240	9476	8747	8438	8068	2888	...	3912	3294	9284
10,974	9300	8985	9944	9310	10,520	9782	7797	9553	10,147	9036	8012	7420	7740	5178	3912	...	4855	9659
6687	7451	5963	6754	7252	6027	6765	5768	6587	6143	6398	5455	5145	4790	732	3294	4855	...	6424
3764	1235	676	366	1057	3738	347	1871	222	4399	653	1654	2253	2037	6601	9284	9659	6424	...

INTERNATIONAL DIALLING CODES

International Access Code + Country Code + City Code + Local Number

To dial direct: First dial the international access code (00). !mmediately thereafter, dial the country code followed by the city code, if applicable, and then the local number, which you must obtain beforehand.

location	country code	city code
AFGHANISTAN	93	
ALBANIA	355	
ALGERIA	213	*
AMERICAN SAMOA	684	*
ANDORRA	33	
ANGOLA	244	
ARGENTINA	54	
Buenos Aires		1
Córdoba		51
Mendoza		61
San Juan		64
Santa Fe		42
ARMENIA	374	
ARUBA	297	
ASCENSION ISLAND	247	
AUSTRALIA	61	
Adelaide		8
Brisbane		7
Gold Coast		75
Melbourne		3
Perth		9
Sydney		2
AUSTRIA	43	
Graz		316
Innsbruck		512
Linz		70
Salzburg		662
Vienna		1
BAHRAIN	973	*
BANGLADESH	880	
Dhaka		2
BELGIUM	32	
Antwerp		3
Brussels		2
Ghent		91
Mons		65
BELIZE	501	
Belize City		2
Punta Gorda		7
San Ignacio		92
BELARUS	375	
BENIN	229	*
BHUTAN	975	*
BOLIVIA	591	
La Paz		2
Santa Cruz de la Sierra		33
BOSNIA AND HERZEGOVINA	387	
BOTSWANA	267	
Gaborone		31
BRAZIL	55	
Brasilia		61
Porto Alegre		512
Rio de Janeiro		21
São Paulo		11
Vitoria		27
BRUNEI	673	
Kuala Belait		3
BULGARIA	359	
Plovdiv		32
Sofia		2
Varna		52
BURKINA FASO	226	*
BURUNDI	257	
Bujumbura		22
CANADA		
CAMBODIA	855	
CAMEROON	237	*
CAPE VERDE ISLANDS	238	*
CENTRAL AFRICAN REPUBLIC	236	
CHAD	235	
CHILE	56	
Concepción		41
Santiago		2
Valparaiso		32
Viña del Mar		32
CHINA	86	
Beijing		1
Shanghai		21
COLUMBIA	57	
Bogotá		1
Cali		23
Cartagena		59
Medellín		4
Palmira		31
CONGO	242	*
COOK ISLANDS	682	*
COSTA RICA	506	*
COTE D'IVOIRE	225	*
CROATIA	385	
CUBA	53	
CYRUS	357	
Nicosia		2
CZECH REPUBLIC	42	
Ostrava		69
Prague		2
DENMARK	45	*
DJIBOUTI	253	*
ECUADOR	593	
Cuenca		7
Esmeraldas		6
Quito		2
EGYPT	20	
Alexandria		3
Aswan		97
Cairo		2
Port Said		66
EL SALVADOR	503	*
EQUATORIAL GUINEA	240	
Malabo		9
ERITREA	291	
ESTONIA	372	
ETHOPIA	251	
Addis Ababa		1
FALKLAND ISLANDS	500	*
FIJI	679	
FINLAND	358	
Helsinki		0
Pori		39
Vaasa		61
FRANCE	33	
Bordeaux		56
Cannes		93
Grenoble		76
Lyon		7
Marseille		91
Nancy		8
Nice		93
Paris		1
Tours		47
FRENCH ANTILLES	596	*
FRENCH GUIANA	594	*
FRENCH POLYNESIA	689	*
F.Y.R.O.M.	389	
GABON	241	*
GAMBIA	220	*
GEORGIA	995	
GERMANY	49	
Berlin		30
Bonn		228
Cologne		221
Dresden		351
Dusseldorf		211
Frankfurt		69
Hamburg		40
Heidelberg		6221
Munich		89
Stuttgart		711
GHANA	233	
Accra		21
GIBRALTAR	350	*
GREECE	30	
Athens		1
Corinth		741
Tripolis		71
GREENLAND	299	
Godthaab		2
GUADELOUPE	590	*
GUANTANAMO BAY	53	99
GUATEMALA	502	
Guatemala City		2
All other cities		9
GUINEA	224	
Conakry		4

* No city codes required. Please note: International dialing codes subject to change without notice.

location	country code	city code
GUYANA	592	
Georgetown		02
HAITI	509	
Port-au-Prince		1
HONDURAS	504	*
HONG KONG	852	
Victoria		5
HUNGARY	36	
Budapest		1
Kaposvar		82
ICELAND	354	
Akureyri		6
Reykjavik		1
INDIA	91	
Bangladore		812
Bhopal		755
Bombay		22
Calcutta		33
Madras		44
New Dehli		11
INDONESIA	62	
Cirebon		231
Denpasar (Bali)		361
Jakarta		21
Malang		341
Semarang		24
IRAN	98	
Tehran		21
IRAQ	964	
Baghdad		1
IRELAND	353	
Cork		21
Dublin		1
Galway		91
Kildare		45
Killarney		64
Tipperary		62
Waterford		51
ISRAEL	972	
Haifa		4
Jerusalem		2
Nazareth		6
Tel Aviv		3
ITALY	39	
Capri		81
Florence		55
Genoa		10
Milan		2
Naples		81
ITALY continued		
Palermo		91
Pisa		50
Rome		6
Venice		41

location	country code	city code
JAPAN	81	
Hiroshima		82
Kyoto		75
Nagasaki		958
Naha (Okinawa)		988
Osaka		6
Toyko		3
Yokohama		45
JORDAN	962	
Amman		6
Jerash		4
KAZAKSTAN	7	
KENYA	254	
Mombasa		11
Nairobi		2
KOREA, NORTH	850	
Pyongyan		2
KOREA, SOUTH	82	
Inhon		336
Pusan		51
Seoul		2
KUWAIT	965	*
KYRGYZSTAN	7	
LAOS	856	
LATVIA	371	
LEBANON	961	
LESOTHO	226	*
LIBERIA	231	*
LIBYA	218	
Tripoli		21
LIECHTENSTEIN	41	75
LITHUANIA	370	
LUXEMBOURG	352	*
MACAO	853	*
MADAGASCAR	261	
Antananarivo		2
MALAWI	265	
Domasi		231
MALAYSIA	60	
Alor Setar		4
Kuala Lumpur		3
Port Dixon		6
MALDIVES	960	*
MALI	223	*
MALTA	356	*
MARSHALL ISLANDS	692	
MARTINIQUE	596	

location	country code	city code
MAURITANIA	222	*
MAURITIUS	230	*
MEXICO	52	
Acapulco		74
Cancun		988
Chihuahua		14
Mexico City		5
Monterrey		83
Puerto Vallarta		322
Veracruz		29
MICRONESIA	691	
MOLDOVA	373	
MONACO	377	93
MOROCCO	21	
Casablanca		2
Marrakech		4
Rabat		7
Tangiers		99
MOZAMBIQUE	258	
Maputo		1
MYANMAR	95	
NAMBIA	264	
Windhoek		61
NEPAL	977	*
NETHERLANDS	31	
Amsterdam		20
Haalem		23
The Hague		70
Rotterdam		10
NETHERLANDS ANTILLES	599	
Curaçao		9
St. Maarten		5
NEW CALEDONIA	687	*
NEW ZEALAND	64	
Auckland		9
Christchurch		3
Wellington		4
NICARAGUA	505	
León		311
Managua		2
NIGER REPUBLIC	227	
NIGERIA	234	
Lagos		1
NORWAY	47	
Oslo		2
OMAN	968	*
PAKISTAN	92	
Islamabad		51
Karachi		21

location	country code	city code
PANAMA	507	*
PAPUA NEW GUINEA	675	
PARAGUAY	595	
Asunción		21
PERU	51	
Arequipa		54
Lima		14
Trujillo		44
PHILIPPINES	63	
Angeles		55
Manila		2
Tarlac		47
POLAND	48	
Gdansk		58
Krakow		12
Poznan		61
Warsaw		22
PORTUGAL	351	
Lisbon		1
Madeira Islands		91
QATAR	974	*
ROMANIA	40	
Bucharest		1
RUSSIA	7	
Moscow		095
St. Petersburg		812
RWANDA	250	*
SAMOA, WESTERN	658	
SAN MARINO	378	549
SAUDI ARABIA	966	
Jeddah		2
Riyadh		3
SENEGAL	221	*
SEYCHELLES	248	*
SIERRA LEONE	232	
Freetown		22
SINGAPORE	65	
SLOVAKIA	42	
SLOVENIA	386	
SOLOMAN ISLANDS	677	
SOMALIA	252	
SOUTH AFRICA	27	
Cape Town		21
Johannesburg		11
Pretoria		12
SPAIN	34	
Barcelona		3
Madrid		1

* No city codes required. Please note: International dialing codes subject to change without notice.

265

location	country code	city code
Seville		5
Valencia		6
SRI LANKA	94	
Colombo		1
SURINAME	597	*
SWAZILAND	268	
SWEDEN	46	
Helsingborg		42
Stockholm		8
Uppsala		18
SWITZERLAND	41	
Baden		56
Bern		31
Geneva		22
Interlaken		36
Lucerne		41
Lugano		91
Zurich		1
SYRIA	963	
Damascus		11
TAIWAN	886	
Chunan		36
Fenguyan		4
Lotung		39
Taipei		2
TAJIKISTAN	7	

location	country code	city code
TANZANIA	255	
Dar es Salaam		51
THAILAND	66	
Bangkok		2
Lampang		54
Tak		55
TONGA	676	
TUNISIA	216	
Tunis		1
TURKEY	90	
Ankara		4
Istanbul		1
Konya		331
Samsun		361
TURKMENISTAN	7	
UGANDA	256	
Entebbe		42
Kampala		41
UKRAINE	380	
UNITED ARAB EMIRATES	971	
Abu Dhabi		2
Ajman		6
Al Ain		3
Dubai		4
Fujairah		70

location	country code	city code
Ras-Al-Khaimah		77
Sharjah		6
Umm-Al-Qaiwain		6
UNITED KINGDOM	44	
Belfast		1232
Cardiff		1222
Edinburgh		131
Glasgow		141
Gloucester		1452
Liverpool		151
London (inner)		171
London (outer)		181
Manchester		161
Nottingham		1602
URUGUAY	598	
Canelones		332
Mercedes		532
Montevideo		2
UZBEKISTAN	7	
VENEZUELA	58	
Barcelona		81
Caracas		2
Ciudad Bolivar		85
Maracaibo		61
Puerto Cabello		42
San Cristobal		76
VIETNAM	84	

location	country code	city code
YUGOSLAVIA	381	
ZAIRE	243	
Kinshasa		12
All other points		2
Zambia	260	
Chingola		2
Kitwe		2
Luanshya		1
Lusaka		2
Ndola		2
ZANZIBAR	259	
ZIMBABWE	263	
Bulawayo		9
Harare		4
Mutare		20

NOTE:

CANADA, BERMUDA, THE CARIBBEAN

To call Canada, Bermuda, and various Caribbean islands like Puerto Rico and the Virgin Islands, International Dialing codes are not employed. Instead, dial only the area code (see the last columns on page 218) plus the local number.

International Access Code + Country Code + City Code + Local Number

Quick reference numbers:-

WEIGHTS AND MEASURES

UNITS OF LENGTH

TO FIND EQUIVALENTS FOR A PARTICULAR UNIT, FIND THE NAME AT THE TOP OF THE APPROPRIATE CHART, READ DOWN THAT COLUMN UNTIL YOU THE BOLD NUMERAL ONE (1), AND THEN READ ACROSS THAT ROW. Numbers with decimals have been rounded to the nearest hundredth, and values above 9,999,999 or below .01 have been omitted.

| U.S. | | | | | | | | | | | METRIC |
miles	furlongs	rods	yards	feet	inches	milli-metres	centi-metres	deci-metres	metres	hecto-metres	kilo-metres
1	8	320	1,760	5,280	63,360	1,609,344	160,934.4	16,093.44	1,609.34	16.09	1.61
.13	1	40	220	660	7,920	201,168	20,116.8	2,011.68	201.16	2.01	.2
	.03	1	5.5	16.5	198	5,029.2	502.92	50.29	5.03	.05	
		.18	1	3	36	914.4	91.44	9.14	.91		
		.06	.33	1	12	304.8	30.48	3.04	.3		
			.03	.08	1	25.4	2.54	.25	.02		
					0.3	1	.1	.01			
			.01	.03	.39	10	1	.1	.01		
		.02	.11	.33	3.94	100	10	1	.1		
		.2	1.09	3.28	39.38	1,000	100	10	1	.01	
.06	.49	19.88	109.36	328.08	3,937.8	100,000	10,000	1,000	100	1	.1
.62	4.96	198.84	1,093.61	3,280.84	39,378	1,000,000	100,000	10,000	1,000	10	1

UNITS OF AREA

| U.S. | | | | | | | | | | | METRIC |
square miles	acres	square rods	square yards	square feet	square inches	sq. milli-metres	sq. centi-metres	sq. deci-metres	square metres	hectares	sq. kilo-metres
1	640	102,400	3,097,600						2,589,988	258.99	2.59
	1	160	4,840	43,560	6,272,640			404,687	4,046.87	.4	
		1	30.25	272.25	39,204		252,929	2,529.29	25.29		
		.03	1	9	1,296	836,127	8,361.27	83.61	.84		
			.11	1	144	92,903	929.03	9.29	.09		
					1	645.16	6.45	.06			
						1	.01				
					.16	100	1	.01			
			.01	.11	15.5	10,000	100	1	.01		
		.04	1.19	10.76	1,550	1,000,000	10,000	100	1	.01	
	2.47	395.37	11,959	107,639				1,000,000	10,000	1	.01
.39	247	39,537	1,195,990						1,000,000	100	1

WEIGHTS AND MEASURES

tons	hundred-weights	pounds	ounces	drams	grains	milli-grams	centi-grams	grams	hecto-grams	kilo-grams	metric tons
1	20	2,000	32,000	512,000				907,184	9,071.85	907.18	.91
.05	1	100	1,600	25,600	699,904		4,535,923	45,359.2	453.59	45.36	.05
	.01	1	16	256	7,000	453,592	45,359	453.59	4.54	.45	
		.06	1	16	437.5	28,349.5	2,834.95	28.35	.28	.03	
			.06	1	27.34	1,771.85	177.19	1.77	.02		
				.04	1	64.8	6.48	.06			
					0.2	1	.1				
					.15	10	1	.01			
			.04	.56	15.43	1,000	100	1	.01		
		.22	3.53	56.44	1,543.24	100,000	10,000	100	1	.1	
	.02	2.2	35.27	564.38	15,432.4	1,000,000	100,000	1,000	10	1	
1.1	22.05	2,204.62	35,274	564,384				1,000,000	10,000	1,000	1

UNITS OF CAPACITY (LIQUID)

U.S.						METRIC					
gallons	quarts	pints	cups	fluid ounces	fluid drams	milli-litres	centi-litres	deci-litres	litres	hecto-litres	kilo-litres
1	4	8	16	128	1,024	3,785.54	378.54	37.85	3.79	.04	
.25	1	2	4	32	256	946.35	94.64	9.46	.95		
.13	.5	1	2	16	128	473.18	47.32	4.73	.47		
.06	.25	.5	1	8	64	236.59	23.65	2.36	.24		
	.03	.06	.13	1	8	29.57	2.96	.29	.03		
			.02	.13	1	3.6	.36	.04			
				0.3	.27	1	.1	.01			
	.01	.02	.04	.34	2.71	10	1	.1	.01		
.03	.11	.21	.42	3.38	27.05	100	10	1	.1		
.26	1.06	2.11	4.23	33.81	270.51	1,000	100	10	1	.01	
26.42	105.67	211.34	422.68	3,381.4	27,051.2	100,000	10,000	1,000	100	1	.1
264.17	1,056.69	2,113.38	4,226.76	33,814	270,512	1,000,000	100,000	10,000	1,000	10	1

WEIGHTS AND MEASURES

UNITS OF LENGTH

1 agate (typography)	=	.07 inch	=	.18 centimetre
1 angstrom	=	.0000001 millimetre	=	.000000004 inch
1 cable's length	=	720 feet	=	219.46 metres
1 chain (engineer's)	=	100 feet	=	30.48 metres
1 chain (Gunter 's or surveyor's)	=	66 feet	=	20.12 metres
1 cubit	=	18 inches	=	45.72 centimetres
1 degree (geographical)	=	69.05 miles	=	111.12 kilometres
1 dekametre	=	10 metres	=	32.81 feet
1 fathom	=	6 feet	=	1.83 metres
1 hand	=	4 inches	=	10.16 centimetres
1 league	=	3 miles	=	4.83 kilometres
1 light-year	=	5,880,000,000,000 miles	=	9,462,684,000,000 kilometres
1 link (Gunter 's or surveyor's)	=	7.92 inches	=	20.12 centimetres
1 link (engineer's)	=	1 foot	=	.31 metre
1 micrometre	=	.001 millimetre	=	.000039 inch
1 micron	=	.001 millimetre	=	.000039 inch
1 mil	=	.001 inch	=	0.3 millimetre
1 millimicron	=	.000001 millimetre	=	.000000039 inch
1 nanometre	=	.000001 millimetre	=	.000000039 inch
1 nautical mile	=	1.15 miles	=	1.852 kilometres
1 perch or pole	=	16.5 feet	=	5 metres
1 point (typography)	=	0.1 inch	=	.35 millimetre

UNITS OF AREA OR SURFACE

1 are	=	100 square metres	=	1,076.39 square feet
1 square (building)	=	100 square feet	=	9.29 square metres
1 square chain	=	4,356 square feet	=	404.69 square metres
1 square link	=	62.73 square inches	=	404.69 square centimetres
1 square perch	=	272.25 square feet	=	25.29 square metres
1 square pole	=	272.25 square feet	=	25.29 square metres
1 township	=	36 square miles	=	93.24 square kilometres

UNITS OF VOLUME

1 cubic inch	=	.00058 cubic foot	=	16.39 cubic centimetres
1 cubic foot	=	1,728 cubic inches	=	28.32 cubic decimetres
1 cubic yard	=	27 cubic feet	=	.76 cubic metre
1 cubic millimetre	=	.001 cubic centimetre	=	.000061 cubic inch
1 cubic centimetre	=	1,000 cubic millimetres	=	.06 cubic inch
1 cubic decimetre	=	1,000 cubic centimetres	=	61.02 cubic inches
1 cubic metre	=	1,000 cubic decimetres	=	35.31 cubic feet
1 stere	=	1 cubic metre	=	35.31 cubic feet

UNITS OF CAPACITY (LIQUID)

1 barrel	=	31 to 42 gallons	=	117.34 to 158.98 litres
1 cubic foot	=	7.48 gallons	=	28.32 litres
1 cubic inch	=	.55 fluid ounce	=	.02 centilitre
1 dekalitre	=	10 litres	=	2.64 gallons
1 gallon (British Imperial)	=	1.20 gallons (U.S.)	=	4.55 litres
1 gill	=	4 fluid ounces	=	.12 centilitre
1 minim	=	.002 fluid ounce	=	.06 millilitre
1 quart (British)	=	1.20 quarts (U.S.)	=	1.14 litres
1 tablespoon	=	.5 fluid ounce	=	1.45 centilitres
1 teaspoon	=	1.33 fluid drams	=	4.92 millilitres

WEIGHTS AND MEASURES

UNITS OF CAPACITY (DRY)

1 barrel (standard)	=	105 quarts	=	115.61 litres
1 barrel (cranberries)	=	86.70 quarts	=	95.46 litres
1 bushel (U.S.), struck measure	=	32 quarts	=	35.24 litres
1 bushel (U.S.), heaped	=	40.9 quarts	=	45.03 litres
1 cubic inch	=	.015 quart	=	.016 litre
1 cord (firewood)	=	128 cubic feet	=	3.62 cubic metres
1 cubic decimetre	=	1 litre	=	.91 quart
1 peck	=	8 quarts	=	8.81 litres
1 pint	=	.5 quart	=	.55 litre
1 quart (U.S.)	=	67.2 cubic inches	=	1.1 litres
1 quart (British)	=	1.032 quarts (U.S.)	=	1.036 litres

UNITS OF WEIGHT OR MASS

1 assay ton	=	29.167 grams	=	1.03 ounces
1 carat	=	200 milligrams	=	3.09 grains
1 decigram	=	100 milligrams	=	1.54 grains
1 dekagram	=	10 grams	=	.35 ounce
1 dram (apothecaries')	=	60 grains	=	3.888 grams
1 gross hundredweight	=	112 pounds	=	50.802 kilograms
1 gross ton	=	2,240 pounds	=	1,016 kilograms
1 long hundredweight	=	112 pounds	=	50.802 kilograms
1 long ton	=	2,240 pounds	=	1,016 metric tons
1 microgram	=	.000001 gram	=	.000000035 ounce
1 ounce (apothecaries')	=	1.097 ounces (avoirdupois)	=	31.10 grams
1 ounce (troy)	=	1.097 ounces (avoirdupois)	=	31.10 grams
1 pennyweight	=	24 grains	=	1.555 grams
1 point	=	.03 grains	=	2 milligrams
1 pound (apothecaries')	=	.823 pound (avoirdupois)	=	.37 kilogram
1 pound (troy)	=	.823 pound (avoirdupois)	=	.37 kilogram
1 scruple (apothecaries')	=	20 grains	=	64.79 milligrams
1 stone	=	14 pounds	=	6.35 kilograms

GEOMETRIC FORMULAS

b = base   C = circumference   d = diameter   h = height   l = length   r = radius   w = width π = 3.1416

Circle
Area = $\pi \times r^2$
Area of sector = $1/2 \, r \times$ length of arc
Circumference = $\pi \times d$ or $2\pi \, xr$
Diameter = $C \div \pi$
Radius = $C \div 2\pi$

Cylinder

Area = l x w

Triangle
Area = $1/2 \, b \times h$

Cone
Volume = $1/3 \, h \times$ (area of the base)

Cylinder or Prism
Volume = h x (area of the base)

Cube or Rectangular Box
Volume = l x w x h

Sphere
Circumference = 3.8978 x (cube root of volume)
Diameter = 1.2407 x (cube root of volume)
Diameter = .56419 x (square root of surface)
Surface area = C x d

Volume = $1/6$ (surface area) x d

STANDARD/METRIC CONVERSIONS

inch	x	25.4	=	millimetre	millimetre	x	.0394	=	inch
foot	x	.3048	=	metre	metre	x	3.2808	=	foot
yard	x	.9144	=	metre	metre	x	1.0936	=	yard
mile	x	1.6093	=	kilometre	kilometre	x	.6214	=	mile
acre	x	.4047	=	hectare	hectare	x	2.4710	=	acre
quart	x	.9463	=	litre	litre	x	1.0567	=	quart
gallon	x	.004	=	cubic metre	cubic metre	x	284.2	=	gallon
ounce	x	28.3495	=	gram	gram	x	.0353	=	ounce
pound	x	.4536	=	kilogram	kilogram	x	2.2046	=	pound
degrees Fahrenheit	x	$5/9 - 32$	=	degrees Celsius	degrees Celsius	x	$9/5 + 32$	=	degrees Fahrenheit